RYAN MCINTOSH

Fear Full

A Biblical & Beautiful Fear of the Lord

First published by Ryan McIntosh 2025

Copyright © 2025 by Ryan McIntosh

All rights reserved. No part of this publication may be reproduced, stored or transmitted in any form or by any means, electronic, mechanical, photocopying, recording, scanning, or otherwise without written permission from the publisher. It is illegal to copy this book, post it to a website, or distribute it by any other means without permission.

Ryan McIntosh has no responsibility for the persistence or accuracy of URLs for external or third-party Internet Websites referred to in this publication and does not guarantee that any content on such Websites is, or will remain, accurate or appropriate.

Scripture quotations are from The ESV® Bible (The Holy Bible, English Standard Version®), copyright © 2001 by Crossway, a publishing ministry of Good News Publishers. Used by permission. All rights reserved.

First edition

ISBN: 979-8-218-63638-8

Editing by Hannah McIntosh
Cover art by Rebekah McIntosh

This book was professionally typeset on Reedsy.
Find out more at reedsy.com

'Twas grace that taught my heart to fear,
And grace my fears relieved
– John Newton

Contents

Preface		ii
1	Does Fear Matter	1
2	A Definition	15
3	Four Fears	20
4	Awesome God	35
5	God's Judgment	54
6	The Authority of Jesus	76
7	Empowerment of the Spirit	99
8	Our Father's Discipline	114
9	The Big Picture	133
Acknowledgments		141
Appendix A: "Fear of the Lord" Bible Verse Commentary		143
Appendix B: "Fear God" Bible Verse Commentary		155
Appendix C: "Fear the Lord" Bible Verse Commentary		162
Appendix D: "Fear of God" Bible Verse Commentary		176
Appendix E: "Fears the Lord" Bible Verse Commentary		181
Notes		185

Preface

Fear Full is primarily for those who would call themselves disciples of Jesus: Those who have put their faith and hope in the name of Jesus, the Son of God, as their Lord and Savior; who died for the sins of the world, was raised from the dead to offer eternal life, ascended to heaven as our perfect high priest, and will return one day in glory. This book is also written for those who are curious about God - who would say that they don't believe in Jesus - yet desire to learn more about what the Bible says about fearing God. I want the following chapters and pages to be clear and accessible to all readers; especially readers that are young and perhaps still in high school or college.

I wrote this book because of the many trials and triumphs that God graciously allowed me to experience; all of which have shown me the importance of fearing God. Coming out of those experiences, I began to take a closer look at what the Bible says about fearing God. As I shared my findings with friends and mentors, they seemed to be as intrigued as I was at this fascinating biblical topic. I began to form a discussion outline for use in a weekly Bible study, and soon discovered that the content for this topic was too extensive to fit into a single weeknight. From that realization, the idea of *Fear Full* was born.

My curiosity lead me to devour dozens of books and online resources on the subject. The more I studied, the more I became convinced that a healthy fear of the Lord is essential to our relationship with him. Over the last few years, learning to fear God how he intends has continually and beneficially transformed my life. I will share my experiences in this book. It has been a joy to embark on this journey of studying and writing about the fear of the Lord.

Although I started strong, my writing and research tapered off a bit due to a season of long-term dating, a short engagement, and the beginning of a wonderful marriage with my lovely wife Hannah. Her intelligence and encouragement have been of great help to me in my renewed endeavor to write this book. I began this project in November 2021. It is now almost half-way through 2025. For years to come, my desire is that *Fear Full* will be an encouraging resource to others in the way it has been to me.

In this short book on the fear of the Lord, I begin by comparing and contrasting generic fear vs. godly fear. I give a definition of a proper fear of the Lord based on Scripture. I delve into the application of fearing God by dividing it into four separate fear categories and providing examples for each from the Bible. Next, I write about being in awe of God's greatness because of who he is and what he has done. I also describe God's judgment on sin and how fear of him should motivate urgency and repentance. I then take a Trinitarian approach to the fear of the Lord - Son, Spirit, and Father. Last of all, I summarize the benefits of fearing the Lord and give a testimony of what God has done in my life though fearing him. I have appendices at the end which contain lists of many Bible verses that pertain to the fear of the Lord along with helpful context for each.

It is my belief that God desires his people to fear him, and that it's for our good. I want my life to be so full of the fear of God that the world will see my life and respond with faith in Jesus.

This is my heartfelt desire for your life as well. The fear of the Lord is not only biblical; but, as I hope you will see throughout this book, it is beautiful as well. Thus my challenge to you is this: Feast on the fear of the Lord as you seek to follow Jesus. Be *Fear Full*.

1

Does Fear Matter

What is the craziest thing you've ever done?

As I consider this question, several memories flash through my mind: Once on a windy day I approached the edge of a mountain cliff with a dizzying drop below. Another time, I recall walking up a hill and watching a massive thunderstorm roll in. I also remember on several occasions advancing toward blazing bonfires just beyond the point of getting singed. More recently, I was at a beach and swam all the way out to a buoy to dive for shells.

One might debate the wisdom of these actions, but I want you to consider these questions: On the windy cliff, what prevented me from leaping over the edge? Before the onset of the thunderstorm, what caused me to seek shelter? In the presence of a fire, why was I not tempted to throw myself into the flames? Or at the beach, why would I not keep swimming out into the ocean as far as possible?

The answer is fear. In each instance, a healthy sense of fear guarded me from crossing lines which would have brought certain harm to myself or threatened my survival. Fear *en-*

hanced these experiences, allowing me to appreciate the wonder of nature while also prompting me to tread lightly with such powerful forces.

The fear of God carries similar benefits. It is my belief that fearing God allows us to enjoy him in a deeper way than before, and keeps us from making a shipwreck of our lives. Fearing God is eternally rewarding.

I imagine that as you read this book, you are coming into it with preconceived notions of fearing God, or fear in general, that inform the way you view life and interact with others. Maybe your views of what fear is have been drilled into you through devastating events in your life, causing you to be frightened by the idea of fearing God. Perhaps you have never thought deeply about God-centered fear, and this topic is intriguing and exciting for you. Wherever you're coming from, or whatever life experience you bring into reading this book, my hope is that it will be like a breath of fresh air or a lifted burden. I want you to revel in the biblical and beautiful fear of the Lord.

***

The purpose of *Fear Full* can be summarized in two words: Fear God. If we broke this sentence down into a diagram, it would look like this:

```
(you)  |  Fear  |  God
_____|_____|_____
       |
```

The sentence "Fear God" is an imperative sentence, which means it is a command or an instruction. Perhaps the first thing that caught your eye was an added word to the diagram: you. The word "you" is the (implied) subject of this imperative sentence. You are the one who is supposed to complete the action. The required action in this command is "fear" and "God" is the sole object or recipient of such an action.

Our discussion of fearing God will follow this same train of thought. In this chapter, our first objective is to examine ourselves and how we relate to fear. We will take a brief look at different definitions of fear and introduce the biblical significance of fearing God. In the next two chapters I'll define fear of the Lord and expound on four types of fear. Finally, we will explore the object of our fear. This includes a couple chapters focusing on God's awesomeness and judgment. Then to conclude our discussion on God, we will spend three chapters on how God-centered fear relates to each distinct person of the Trinity: Son, Spirit, and Father. The overarching purpose of our study is to discern who God is and what it means to fear him.

Examining Ourselves

Who are you as a person? Who are we as people? If we are to understand fearing God, we must understand our natural tendency toward unhealthy fearful dispositions. Taking a quick survey of our lives, it becomes apparent that we don't fear God as much as we fear other things. Specifically in the United States we are a fearful bunch. Author Michael Reeves has noted, "These days, it seems, everyone is talking about a culture of fear."[1] Unfortunately, this quote is backed by research. In the *Chapman University Survey of American Fears (2020/2021)*, it was discovered that the top ten fears of Americans were as follows[2]:

1. Corrupt government officials - **79.6% very afraid or afraid**
2. People I love dying - **58.5% very afraid or afraid**
3. A loved one contracting the coronavirus (COVID-19) - **58% very afraid or afraid**
4. People I love becoming seriously ill - **57.3% very afraid or afraid**
5. Widespread civil unrest - **56.5% very afraid or afraid**
6. A pandemic or a major epidemic - **55.8% very afraid or afraid**
7. Economic/financial collapse - **54.8% very afraid or afraid**
8. Cyber-terrorism - **51% very afraid or afraid**
9. Pollution of oceans, rivers, and lakes - **50.8% very afraid or afraid**
10. Biological warfare - **49.3% very afraid or afraid**

Do any of these things cause you to be afraid? I can personally see how these fears impact my life and the lives of those around me. Living with these fears raises our anxiety and affects our mental health. It influences where we choose to live and who we vote for. These fears tell us what groceries to buy and how much to stock up in case of disasters. They are also projected onto the internet through our stories and status updates. To further complicate the issue, people come along who monetize and weaponize the fears of others. It's a mess.

Living in fear is not confined to the borders of the USA. Around the world, many countries fall under the category of having *fear-power cultures*. Cultural expert Jayson Georges explains fear-power cultures like this:

> Fear-power cultures live in constant fear of invisible powers. They fear a potential misstep may open a vulnerable point for spiritual influence or expose them to harm – such as an accident, a bad dream, or even possession. People in fear-based contexts never know what evil the capricious spirits might inflict. To control the unknowns of life and ward off evil influences, they resort to magical rituals. Secret techniques harness spiritual power to avoid harm and invite blessings. People strive to live in peace with the forces that cohabitate their world. Disharmony with the spiritual could prove disastrous.[3]

The conclusion we must come to informs us that fear is globally inseparable from the human experience. Our first example of fear in human history occurs in the garden of Eden. Here we see a fallen Adam fearful and hiding from God: "And he said, 'I heard the sound of you in the garden, and I was afraid, because

I was naked, and I hid myself' " (Genesis 3:10).

Furthermore, our rampant fear is not dependent on privilege or status. Even a rich and healthy individual with a happy family in a time of peace will succumb to fear. Fear drives every person in every place in every era. Take a second and try to imagine a world where people weren't driven by their fears. *No fear of being robbed. No fear of the stock market crashing. No fear of health crises. No fear of relationship loss.* You'll quickly realize that this is impossible. Our fears are intertwined with our identity. In our sinful disposition, we fear the things of this world more than we fear God.

Generic Fear Defined

At this point, we must ask the question: What is fear? According to Merriam-Webster dictionary, the essential meaning of fear is "an unpleasant emotion caused by being aware of danger" or "a feeling of respect and wonder for something very powerful."[4] These definitions are important because we will build from them to help us understand fearing God. I want to label these two definitions as 'generic fear'.

Both definitions infer that fear is emotional. You will find that if you ever have a fearful thought or a fearful decision, it is rooted in the emotion of fear. The emotion of fear is strong and can feed into our actions and worldviews.

The first definition of generic fear is "an unpleasant emotion caused by being aware of danger." An awareness of perceived danger causes the feeling of fear. This definition of generic fear can lead us to a fear of God because God is dangerous. The Bible teaches in Exodus 33:20 that the mere presence of God would kill us. God threatens the selfish thrones and idols we erect in our lives. He actively reigns over us whether we acknowledge him or not. His presence shakes us to the very core. A.W. Tozer writes of fear,

> In olden days men of faith were said to 'walk in the fear of God' and to 'serve the Lord with fear.' However intimate their communion with God, however bold their prayers, at the base of their religious life was the conception of God as awesome and dreadful. This idea of God transcendent rims through the whole Bible and gives color and tone to the character of the saints. This fear of God was more than a natural apprehension of danger; it was a nonrational dread, an acute feeling of personal insufficiency in the presence of God the Almighty.[5]

Even if, as our definition suggests, you are fearful of something due to an awareness of danger, that does not mean the danger is actually present. This distinction brings us to a discussion of fear and anxiety. Are they the same thing? According to a study published in Behavior Therapy, over the course of thirty days, "91.4% of worry predictions did not come true"[6] for the twenty-nine study participants with generalized anxiety disorder. For these individuals, less than one-tenth of their fears came to fruition over the course of a month! I wonder how often this is the case for us.

While anxiety is a very real experience, it is different from fear. According to Psychology Today, "Fear and anxiety are very closely related and both contain the idea of danger or the possibility of injury. In general, fear is seen as a reaction to a perception of threat posed by a specific, observable danger. Anxiety, however, is seen as diffuse, a kind of unfocused, objectless, future-oriented feeling. Thus, fear is a perception that is attached to a specific thing, thought or circumstance."[7] McLean Hospital summarizes this more succinctly by saying that fear "is the response to a perceived threat, while anxiety involves worry about a threat that has not yet, or may never, happen."[8] If you find yourself being worried about something that is not real or present, it may be anxiety rather than fear. This is an important distinction to help us understand what fear is not.

Rest assured, if you are experiencing anxiety in your life, there is hope. Many resources - such as books, churches, and counselors - are available to you. However, the focus of this book is fear. The bottom line is that we may have fears in our lives (such as real punishment, real loss, real pain, or real rejection) that *are* dangerous or deeply hurtful; causing the unpleasant emotion of fear.

Our second definition of generic fear is to experience "a feeling of respect and wonder for something very powerful." Note that this definition of fear doesn't specify that the emotion is unpleasant (as is the case with the first definition). This fear may posit the idea of honor or reverence. With this fear, you are recognizing something or someone's power over you, and posturing yourself around that recognition.

This definition implies that there is an object of your feeling similar to the emotion of love. You cannot love nothing. You may love people. You may love your job or your possessions. You may love God. It is the same with fear. This fear implies the existence of something external to you which you perceive to have power over you. Is it your boss? The government? Your parents? What about God?

So we see again that generic fear can be directed toward God. Scripture tells us that the God of the Bible is all-knowing (omniscient), all-present (omnipresent), and all-powerful (omnipotent). God is infinite, and so God's power is infinite. It is therefore fitting and appropriate to fear God in respect and wonder; in reverence and awe. We will cover this topic in chapter 4.

Generic definitions of fear are helpful in laying a groundwork for understanding fear of the Lord, but I want to make a case here that fear of the Lord should supersede every other fear in our lives. Suppose someone spent their entire life fearing everything but God. They could fear events, actions, or people that threaten their lives or their comfort. They may fear not having enough and so they toil endlessly for money and wealth. Or they might fear the opinions of others, so they people please for decades in order to earn a positive reputation. These are just a few examples. These fears lead them to a seemingly safe and secure existence.

It sounds like this fear leads to a good life right? They gain approval, safety, security, comfort, and wealth - all because they feared everything other than God. Do you know what this kind of fear can never do for them? Generic fear will never change their heart. Generic fear - a human fear - cannot overcome sin, and will not lead to eternal life. Only the fear of the Lord can change the heart, overcome sin, and lead to eternal life through faith in Jesus Christ. What we want to do is elevate our fear so that it is directed primarily toward God.

Charles Spurgeon has said that our fear, when directed toward God and empowered by God, can become the most wonderful part of our lives: "Fear may be used for the most sinful purposes; at the same time it may be so ennobled by grace, and so used for the service of God, that it may become the very grandest part of man. In fact, Scripture has honored fear, for the whole of piety is comprehended in these words, 'Fear God;' 'the fear of the Lord;' 'them that fear Him.' These phrases are employed to express true piety, and the men who possess it."[9]

Purpose in Fearing God

Thus far, we have observed the relationship that humans have with fear, and also the two definitions of generic fear. Fear is an emotion based on the awareness of danger or a reverence for what is powerful. We must now turn to our specific topic: the fear of God. Why is learning to fear God worth our time?

The English Standard Version translation of the Bible - and the translation I'll reference throughout this book - repeats the phrases "fear of the Lord" 27 times, "fears the Lord" 8 times, "fear the Lord" 32 times, "fear of God" 10 times, and "fear God" 15 times. This is not exhaustive as there are other phrases in the Bible that point to the idea of fearing God; but if we just take these numbers, it seems that the Bible delves into the topic at least 92 times!

Yet, when is the last time you heard a sermon or podcast on the topic of fearing God? If all Scripture is "breathed out by God and profitable for teaching, for reproof, for correction, and for training in righteousness" (2 Timothy 3:16), then should we not address this lengthy topic that God has intentionally placed in his Word? These 92 instances in Scripture on the topic of fearing God, in both the Old and New Testaments, should cause us to consider if we are minimizing something that God desires for us.

Within the Bible, the Hebrew word used in the Old Testament for fear is *yir'a* which translates to fear, but it can also mean to "be terrified of" or "to revere". I find this useful as we continue throughout the rest of the book. In addition, the New Testament has a Greek word that is used for fear: *phobos*. This is where we get our word phobia. Phobos carries the additional meanings of "dread" or "fright".

The book of Ecclesiastes was presumably written by Solomon, the son of David and a king of Israel as recorded in the Old Testament. King Solomon was known for his wisdom and riches, both of which were given to him by God. The theme of Ecclesiastes can be described with one word: *vanity*. Throughout the book, Solomon outlined his indulgence in every pleasure under the sun, and how it was all meaningless. Yet, in the very last chapter, after all his observations about the toils of mankind, King Solomon had this to say:

> The end of the matter; all has been heard. Fear God and keep his commandments, for this is the whole duty of man. For God will bring every deed into judgment, with every secret thing, whether good or evil. (Ecclesiastes 12:13-14)

The whole duty.

Solomon's case is summarized in a call to fear God and obey God. Solomon is saying here that fearing God and keeping his commands is *not* vanity, *not* toil, and *not* meaningless; as opposed to everything else he had previously mentioned. It is our duty - a responsibility placed upon us. Why does Solomon say we should fear God and keep his commands? Because God is our judge, and nothing in our lives is overlooked by him.

Solomon is also the presumed author of the book of Proverbs; a book filled with principles about seeking wisdom and living righteously. "The fear of the LORD prolongs life, but the years of the wicked will be short" (Proverbs 10:27), he writes. And "By the fear of the LORD one turns away from evil" (Proverbs 16:6). Do you desire life? What kind of life do you want? A good life? A long life? How about an eternal life perhaps? God's Word is telling us that if we forsake fearing God and instead pursue wickedness, our life will ultimately be cut short. Fearing God is what enables us to turn away from evil.

Fearing God is not just an Old Testament subject. Paul's final letter to the Corinthian church says this:

> Since we have these promises, beloved, let us cleanse ourselves from every defilement of body and spirit, bringing holiness to completion in the fear of God.
> (2 Corinthians 7:1)

Paul is making a correlation between fearing God and living a holy life. If we are to completely step into the holiness that God desires for us, then we must learn to fear God. We must proactively evade the defilement of sin.

Commands to "fear God" are abundant in Scripture, and I quickly want to address some confusion with other commands related to fear in the Bible. In the Old and New Testaments, the phrase "do *not* fear" appears 35 times, "fear *not*" appears 33 times, and "do *not* be afraid" also appears 33 times (emphasis added). So which is it? Are we to fear God, or are we to have no fear? At first glance these statements can seem contradictory, but what I've gleaned from all the verses that contain "do not fear" and "do not be afraid" is that the message is indeed coherent: In general, each of these instances of "don't fear or be afraid" convey that we should not fear uncertainty, or suffering, or death, or nations and armies, or being judged by others. This is why the phrases "do not fear" and "fear God" go hand-in-hand. Scripture never teaches us to *not* fear God.[10]

The biblical principle of "fear God and fear not" is most clearly found in Jesus' words from the Gospel of Luke:

> I tell you, my friends, do not fear those who kill the body, and after that have nothing more that they can do. But I will warn you whom to fear: fear him who, after he has killed, has authority to cast into hell. Yes, I tell you, fear him! Are not five sparrows sold for two pennies? And not one of them is forgotten before God. Why, even the hairs of your head are all numbered. Fear not; you are of more value than many sparrows. (Luke 12:4-7)

Jesus wants his followers to know that we must fear God; but at the same time, we must not fear anything else. Misplaced fear is entirely inappropriate. I am reminded of the words of Paul, "If God is for us, who can be against us?" (Romans 8:31b). Fear God and fear not.

In conclusion, humanity is fearful and distraught. We generally fear the wrong things. Learning to fear God is vital, and it does have a purpose. It matters because from the moment we are born we are prone to fear lesser things. It matters because God is dangerous and awe inspiring. It matters because God's Word is overflowing with commands to fear him. It is our God-given duty. If we are to live a life of holiness and turn away from evil, then we must have a God-centered fear.

If fearing the Lord is crucial for us as humans, then it begs the following question: What does it mean to fear the Lord?

2

A Definition

In the process of writing this book, I have read many books and articles, listened to various sermons, and consumed a number of interviews all related to the topic of fearing the Lord. With all humility, I must confess that many of them are more scholarly and come from more life experience than I am able to offer here. And yet, as a result of my studies, I am convinced that *Fear Full* does have something unique to offer.

When it comes to the fear of the Lord, one thing that I craved was a simple and practical definition. There are countless definitions for the fear of the Lord out there, and yet, from what I have found, none have been holistic in scope or accessible to the average reader. Therefore, upon studying what the Bible has to say on the topic of the fear of God, supplementing that with Christian literature and inviting the input of wise counsel, I have compiled a definition of the fear of the Lord that I pray is helpful to my readers:

> *A proper fear of the Lord is a personal response to being in awe of God's greatness; or being convicted by God's*

chastisement, in which someone is led by the Holy Spirit to know God and love him in a deeper way than before; resulting in gained wisdom, blessings, joy, reverence for God, and obedience to God.

For the rest of this short chapter we will unpack this definition:

A *proper fear of the Lord* - As we will see in the next chapter, there are ways of fearing God that do not breed spiritual health. Some people who fear God are downright wicked. What I mean by a "proper" fear is a fear that transcends the way we fear anything lesser than God. Fearing God is distinctly different from fearing anything or anyone else. I believe this is why the concept of fearing God can be so difficult to grasp or pin down. A proper fear of God that is healthy and right is based on Scripture.

God's Word is not sparing in its revelations about how we are to fear him and why. If you want an idea of just how thoroughly this idea is explained, take a look at the appendices at the back of the book. It is fascinating that God created us to fear him. If we don't learn to fear God on his terms, then we are not stepping into his design for our lives.

is a personal response - Fearing God must be something that is deeply personal. Not only that, but it must be an intentional response on our part. Our fear of God is of a personal God who has revealed himself to us. Our fear of him should not be cold or distant.

Imagine you were trapped in a burning building, and a firefighter came in and pulled you out. Would you not respond by embracing him and thanking him with gratitude and tears? In a similar way, we must respond personally to our God who has done great things for us.

to being in awe of God's greatness - Our proper response of fearing God is prompted by God's attributes and actions. To put it another way, we should be awestruck by God for who he is and what he has done. Jerry Bridges writes, "A profound sense of awe toward God is undoubtedly the dominant element in the attitude or set of emotions that the Bible calls 'the fear of God'."[11]

We respond to God in proper fear when we are awestruck by his greatness. We wonder at his holiness, we marvel at his creation, we ponder all his works, and we tremble at his power. We are amazed and inspired when we behold him.

Think of the best fireworks display you've ever seen. What feeling did it evoke in you as you saw the sky enveloped in color and felt the thunderous booms pounding through your chest? In a similar sense, the experience of who God is and what he has done should leave us awestruck.

or being convicted by God's chastisement - God's chastisement takes two forms: judgment and discipline. The lost person should fear God's righteous judgment of their sin. The saved person should fear God's loving discipline and correction when they aren't living like Christ. Both are meant to evoke a fear of God that convicts us of our sin; enabling us to reject it and turn toward God. This will be fleshed out further in the next chapter and throughout the book.

in which someone is led by the Holy Spirit - This is a humbling thought, but truthfully we cannot respond to God in proper fear unless we are helped by his Spirit. The role of the Holy Spirit will be discussed in detail in chapter 7, but it brings up a point that is well worth noting here: We can only have God's Spirit working in our hearts if we have placed our faith and trust in Jesus the Son of God as our Lord and Savior. This means that only followers of Christ can have a proper fear of the Lord. Yet even we who are believers in Jesus must have a humble attitude and seek to honor Christ so that we do not quench or grieve his Spirit.

Romans 8:8-9a says, "Those who are in the flesh cannot please God. You, however, are not in the flesh but in the Spirit, if in fact the Spirit of God dwells in you." I will say it again: Without the Holy Spirit guiding us, we cannot fear God how he intends. Attempting to rightly fear God without being led by his Spirit inside of you is futile and unsustainable.

to know God and love him in a deeper way than before - This is a very important point. A proper fear of the Lord leads to desiring a deeper knowledge of him and a closer relationship with him. In order for your fear to be healthy, love for God MUST be present and increasing in your heart. Paul writes in 1 Corinthians 13:2, "If I have all faith, so as to remove mountains, but have not love, I am nothing." In a similar way, attempting to fear God rightly without loving him, means that your fear means nothing. Hear these words from John Bunyan:

> If the fear that you have does not unite your heart to God and to the love of his Son, the Bible, and his people, your fear is worth nothing. Many are forced to fear God as slaves are forced to fear their masters. But this is only a false fear. It is not the result of a love for God. This fear does not cause a willing submission. It is not the childlike fear that honors God.[12]

resulting in gained wisdom, blessings, joy, reverence for God, and obedience to God - The Bible is filled with verses that talk about the benefits of fearing the Lord: The fear of the Lord gives you wisdom and knowledge from God. The fear of the Lord leads to abundant life. The fear of the Lord keeps you from turning to evil and sin. The fear of the Lord changes your heart to obey him and delight in him. I could go on.

Essentially, the proper fear of God is meant to be a blessing to us and to bring glory to our Creator. I believe that God uses this fear as a means of sanctifying his people. Bible.org says that, "When we truly fear the Lord, we have union between mind (what we think), heart (what we value and treasure), and body (what we do)."[13] We become like Christ. People who rightly fear God are people who seek to obey God. I have found this to be the case in my own life, and it has been both liberating and beautiful.

Hopefully, this definition has been clarifying as we delve into a deeper understanding of fearing God. In the next chapter we will define healthy and unhealthy ways of fearing God and give examples. Before turning the page, you might find it helpful to review the definition set forth in this chapter, as it will be useful throughout this book and in your own heart and mind.

3

Four Fears

Despite my best attempt to define the fear of the Lord in the last chapter, I know that there will be some inevitable questions, such as, "How does this fear affect my relationship with God?" and, "What are examples of how or how not to fear the Lord?"

In this chapter, I want to dive into what the fear of the Lord actually looks like on a categorical level. This will do one of two things. Ideally, it should impart confidence that how we are fearing the Lord is proper and good. Conversely, if we aren't fearing him in an appropriate way, then this chapter serves as a means of course correction. In my own life, I have required this course correction at times. My fear of God had to undergo metamorphosis to more closely resemble that which is proper and right; biblical and beautiful.

From my study of Scripture, the ways we fear God can be categorized into four fears. These fears can be distinguished by two questions. Is your fear of God due to his greatness or his chastisement? Secondly, is your fear of God healthy or unhealthy? With our fears being healthy or unhealthy – based on God's greatness or his chastisement – we have a matrix of four fears which will be the basis of this chapter:

FOUR FEARS OF GOD	Greatness	Chastisement
Healthy	Healthy Fear of God's Greatness	Healthy Fear of God's Chastisement
Unhealthy	Unhealthy Fear of God's Greatness	Unhealthy Fear of God's Chastisement

What determines if our fear of God is healthy or unhealthy? The answer is three-fold. First, healthy fear of God originates from faith in God. Unhealthy fear originates from doubting God. Faith "is the assurance of things hoped for, the conviction of things not seen" (Hebrews 11:1). Doubt breeds double-mindedness and instability (James 1:8). Doubt doesn't believe in God's promises. It whispers, as the crafty serpent did in the Garden of Eden, "Did God really say so? Certainly not." Faith trusts in the goodness of God. If our fear of God is paired with doubt, it is unhealthy. However, if our fear of God is linked together with faith in God, then our fear is healthy.

Second, healthy fear of God is always accompanied by love for God. In order to be in right relationship with God, and fear him accurately, we must love him with all our heart, soul, mind, and strength (Mark 12:30). This begins by recognizing the love that God has for us. Psalm 147:11 says, "But the LORD takes pleasure in those who fear him, in those who hope in his steadfast love." This verse is equating a hope in God's love to a fear of him. God is pleased with those who fear him and hope in his steadfast love.

Any love for God that we have must be motivated by the love that he has already shown to us. In 1 John 4:19, it says that "We love because he first loved us." Fear of God that is absent of love for God will be rooted in anger, hate, and selfishness. Healthy fear must originate from love.

Finally, healthy fear of God brings us closer to God, while unhealthy fear of God pushes us further from God. Dr. Dan Allender once wrote, "To fear God does not drive us away from God, but rather to God."[14] This is what I would classify as healthy fear. Anyone with a healthy fear of God, upon experiencing God's greatness or chastisement in any capacity, will be compelled to draw nearer to God; to seek him in a more intimate way. While healthy fear brings us closer to God, unhealthy fear causes us to pull away from him. The Jewish Encyclopedia emphasizes this point:

> Fear of God does not make men shrink from Him as one would from a tyrant or a wild beast; it draws them nearer to Him and fills them with reverential awe. That fear which is merely self-regarding is unworthy of a child of God.[15]

So what of the other two fears? What is the difference between God's greatness and God's chastisement? God's greatness refers to anything about him that causes us to have awe or reverence for him. These would include his glory, holiness, creation, loving kindness, power, salvation, knowledge, and his works. If something about God causes you to marvel at him, then this is fear of his greatness.

The fear of God's chastisement is associated with the punishment of sinners and discipline of his children. A perfect God who loves justice must punish sin. A perfect Father who loves his children disciplines them for their own good. Those who do not put their faith in Jesus are not God's children. They fall under God's eternal judgment of sin. Thus, the fear of God's chastisement has a twofold purpose: to keep his children from sinning and cause lost sinners to forsake their sin and turn to God in faith.

In addition to these four categories I have outlined, there is also the possibility that someone will not fear God. In this case, the person is set against God. They seek to oppose God and deny him. In the Bible, Psalm chapter 2 and Romans chapter 1 both describe this type of person. They are rebellious and seek freedom from the goodness, sovereignty, and love of God. Scripture is clear that God's wrath is kindled against them. This foolish person falls under God's judgment unless they turn to him in healthy fear.

Learning to categorize and spot these fears in your own life is important. Do you fear God? What makes you fear God? Is your fear of God healthy? As you continue reading it is worth evaluating which types of fear mark your life. The following biblical examples serve as real life illustrations of how these fears play out.

Fear of God's Greatness

Scripture is loaded with stories of people fearing the greatness of God. Some of these we will cover in chapter 6. For now, I want to surface one positive example of healthy fear that we can learn from:

> But Saul, still breathing threats and murder against the disciples of the Lord, went to the high priest and asked him for letters to the synagogues at Damascus, so that if he found any belonging to the Way, men or women, he might bring them bound to Jerusalem. Now as he went on his way, he approached Damascus, and suddenly a light from heaven shone around him. And falling to the ground, he heard a voice saying to him, "Saul, Saul, why are you persecuting me?" And he said, "Who are you, Lord?" And he said, "I am Jesus, whom you are persecuting. But rise and enter the city, and you will be told what you are to do." (Acts 9:1-6)

Saul, also known as Paul the Apostle, started out as a Pharisee and enemy of Christ. He gave approval of the execution of Stephen and he dragged Christians into prison. He was committed to the persecution of believers. He was zealous to end the faith that he had deemed heretical.

Then, on his journey to Damascus in Syria, Saul was confronted by Jesus in all his glory. As the text says, Saul saw a light from heaven. But this was not just any light, it was the Light of the World. Jesus, in all his radiance and holiness, appeared to a man doing his best to extinguish such light. Saul would later describe what he saw as "brighter than the sun" (Acts 26:13). Later in life he would write in 1 Corinthians 15:8, "Last of all, as to one untimely born, he [Jesus] appeared also to me."

Imagine seeing the resurrected glory of Jesus. What an awesome experience! Saul went straight to the ground with reverence and wonder and fear. This encounter with Jesus blinded him. Yet, Saul responded in a healthy fear; with faith and obedience. He entered Damascus as Jesus commanded. After three days of Saul being blind, God sent Ananias to him:

> So Ananias departed and entered the house. And laying his hands on him he said, "Brother Saul, the Lord Jesus who appeared to you on the road by which you came has sent me so that you may regain your sight and be filled with the Holy Spirit." And immediately something like scales fell from his eyes, and he regained his sight. Then he rose and was baptized; and taking food, he was strengthened. For some days he was with the disciples at Damascus. And immediately he proclaimed Jesus in the synagogues, saying, "He is the Son of God." (Acts 9:17-20)

To summarize: after Saul (aka Paul) had a fearful encounter with the glorified Son of God, he responded in personal faith and obedience to the words of Jesus. Paul started seeking after Jesus and telling other Jews about him.

This is what healthy fear of God's greatness looks like. We experience or learn about God's awesome attributes or actions, and this prompts us to draw near to him in reverence and fear. We draw near to God through our mediator Jesus Christ.

* * *

On the flip side is an unhealthy fear of God's greatness. Unhealthy fear pushes us away from God. It refuses to accept God's mediator that allows us to draw near. Unhealthy fear rightly acknowledges the holiness and might of God, but seeks to separate from him instead of unite with him through a mediator.

In the New Testament, our perfect mediator for all time is Jesus Christ. In the Old Testament, one of the mediators who was a type of Christ was Moses. When Moses and the Israelites were at Mount Sinai, the Israelites exhibited unhealthy fear:

> Now when all the people saw the thunder and the flashes of lightning and the sound of the trumpet and the mountain smoking, the people were afraid and trembled, and they stood far off and said to Moses, "You speak to us, and we will listen; but do not let God speak to us, lest we die." Moses said to the people, "Do not fear, for God has come to test you, that the fear of him may be before you, that you may not sin." The people stood far off, while Moses drew near to the thick darkness where God was. (Exodus 20:18-21)

This all occurred right after God gave them the Ten Commandments. There are a few things to notice from this account. First, the people didn't want to stick around for God's display of his power and glory on the mountain. They were afraid of God's greatness. Second, God wanted them to experience his greatness and know his law, so that through this testing they would learn to fear him in a healthy way. Third, Moses was the one who went directly to God on their behalf.

The text says twice that the people stood far off. I submit that not only were their bodies far off from the mountain of God, but their hearts were far off as well. This was because they had an unhealthy fear of God's greatness.

Why do I suspect that their fear was unhealthy? In Exodus 32, just a few weeks after this event, the Israelites fashioned an idol in the shape of a golden calf. They began sacrificing to it and worshiping it, directly violating the commands that God personally delivered to them. They did not respond to the display of God's greatness in faith. They refused to draw near to God. Their own words show that they rejected the mediator, Moses, that God had given to them: "Up, make us gods who shall go before us. As for this Moses, the man who brought us up out of the land of Egypt, we do not know what has become of him" (Exodus 32:1b). This idolatry was the result of their unhealthy fear of God's greatness.

Fear of God's Chastisement

The Bible also contains many examples of fearing God's chastisement. This is a fear that encompasses judgment and discipline. The lost person should fear God's judgment of their sin. The saved person should fear God's loving discipline and correction.

With a healthy fear of God's chastisement, the lost person will fall under conviction and repent before God. A saved person with healthy fear will seek to walk closely with God and honor him through obedience. An unhealthy fear of God's chastisement will cause the lost person to harden their heart and turn away from God. Likewise, the saved person who has an unhealthy fear of God is immature and will be driven by sin and shame.

Perhaps the most poignant example of a healthy response to God's discipline is King David. This is recounted in 2 Samuel chapters 11 and 12. In this well-known passage, we find King

David in his palace in Jerusalem at a time when he should have been with his army at war.

During this time, David decided one day to take a stroll on the roof of his palace. From this vantage point, he could see the city below, and he noticed a woman bathing. Instead of averting his eyes and removing himself from this tempting position, he continued to observe that she was very beautiful. Succumbing to his desire, David had her brought to his palace and slept with her. As a result, she became pregnant. This woman's name was Bathsheba, and David had just committed adultery with her.

Bathsheba happened to already be married to an honorable warrior named Uriah. Long story short, David ordered that Uriah be killed in order to cover up Bathsheba's pregnancy. Not only did David commit murder here, but in order to pull it off, he also had to be deceitful. Now King David had three strikes against him: adultery, murder, and deceit. What's worse is that David thought he had gotten away with it. Yet nothing escapes God's eyes.

So far, David had shown no fear of God's chastisement, but that was about to change. God sent the prophet Nathan to confront David on his sin. When faced with the evil he had committed, David finally confessed his guilt before God. Even though these sins were deserving of death, David was graciously spared. However, God pronounced that because of these sins, David's own family would rise up against him with the same sort of evil (this is fulfilled later by his son Absalom). Moreover, God told David that the child born to Bathsheba would die.

What does this story have to do with a healthy fear of God's chastisement? The answer is David's response to his punishment. After Bathsheba's son died, David "went into the house of the LORD and worshiped" (2 Samuel 12:20). Not only that, but David penned a beautiful Psalm; the epitome of a healthy response to God's chastisement. Here in Psalm 51 we see the humility and repentance of David's heart:

> Create in me a clean heart, O God, and renew a right spirit within me. Cast me not away from your presence, and take not your Holy Spirit from me. Restore to me the joy of your salvation, and uphold me with a willing spirit. (Psalm 51:10-12)

David, in response to God's chastisement, shows us what healthy fear looks like. Even before the punishment had been fully dealt to David, he *repented* of his sin, he *worshiped* God and he *begged* God to be near him.

Is this how you respond when God disciplines you? When your sins are found out, do you draw near to him? As God reveals and confronts our sin, we should humble ourselves, repent, and worship. Rather than distancing ourselves from God, we must earnestly surrender our hearts to him.

* * *

Since we have seen David's healthy response to God's chastisement, let's look at an unhealthy example. Again, there are many biblical examples, but the one I want to showcase is in Genesis 3; the fall of man.

The setting is the garden of Eden. In the previous chapters, God had created all things and declared it very good. God fashioned Adam and Eve, the first man and woman, to live in the garden of Eden where they were to tend the garden, multiply, and commune with God. There were many trees in the garden, but God had commanded them to not eat of the tree of the knowledge of good and evil. To do so would constitute sin, which would result in death and separation from God.

Then a serpent came to Eve and tempted her to disobey God by eating fruit from the tree. Eve gave into her own desire and ate from the tree. She then gave the fruit to Adam and he partook as well. At that moment, sin entered the world.

Up until this point, Adam and Eve had been naked and felt no shame, but now due to their sin they felt exposed. The tree of the knowledge of good and evil had given them just that – the knowledge that they had chosen what was evil. Driven by their shame, they crafted garments of leaves to cover their nakedness. What they did next was indicative of the separation that now existed between them and God:

> And they heard the sound of the LORD God walking in the garden in the cool of the day, and the man and his wife hid themselves from the presence of the LORD God among the trees of the garden. But the LORD God called to the man and said to him, "Where are you?" And he said, "I heard the sound of you in the garden, and I was afraid, because I was naked, and I hid myself." He said, "Who told you that you were naked? Have you eaten of the tree of which I commanded you not to eat?"
> (Genesis 3:8-11)

Not only did Adam and Eve hide from God because they were afraid, but they went on to blame others for their sinful actions. Although the text says that they were "afraid", we know that healthy fear of God does not lead to distancing from him and blaming others. Adam and Eve were exhibiting unhealthy fear of him.

Even in their sin and unhealthy fear, God was still gracious and loving toward them. He sought them out in their hiding. He did not immediately put them to death for their sins, but instead he killed an animal and covered them with its skin in place of the crude leaf coverings they had made for themselves.[16]

On a practical level for us today, as we consider these stories and continue to pursue healthy fear of the Lord, remember that he is gracious and loving. This is the key truth that keeps us from hiding our sin, blaming others, and distancing ourselves from God. Healthy fear of God's chastisement will bring our hearts closer to God and will grow our desire to avoid sin.

No Fear of God

> as it is written:
> "None is righteous, no, not one; no one understands; no one seeks for God…"
> "There is no fear of God before their eyes."
> (Romans 3:10–11, 18)

It may be difficult to imagine, but there are those who do not fear God. This is neither a healthy or an unhealthy fear of God. It is no regard for him at all. Such people have made themselves their own gods.

Typically, having no fear of God means that someone's heart is so hardened that they are convinced God doesn't exist. Or, on the flip side, they believe that God exists but conclude that he is all loving and not just. Both types of people assume that there is no fear in sinning. To one, God doesn't exist or care and so they need not fear him. To the other, God is all loving so they don't have to fear his wrath. Both disregard God and sin how they please.

A biblical example of someone who didn't fear God was King Ahab. Ahab was a king of Israel during the divided kingdom period. Look at how Scripture records the reign of King Ahab:

> And Ahab the son of Omri did evil in the sight of the LORD, more than all who were before him. And as if it had been a light thing for him to walk in the sins of Jeroboam the son of Nebat, he took for his wife Jezebel the daughter of Ethbaal king of the Sidonians, and went and served Baal and worshiped him. He erected an altar for Baal in the house of Baal, which he built in Samaria. And Ahab made an Asherah. Ahab did more to provoke the LORD, the God of Israel, to anger than all the kings of Israel who were before him.
> (1 Kings 16:30-33)

This is the epitome of not fearing God. King Ahab led the nation in excessive idol worship. The passage says that he delved deeper into evil than all the kings before him - including Jeroboam. He worshiped and promoted false gods imported from surrounding countries. He married an idolatrous pagan woman who enticed him into more wickedness. His heart was full of sin.

We are told that his wife Jezebel killed most of the true prophets of God (1 Kings 18:13). 1 Kings 21:25-26a also tells us that, "There was none who sold himself to do what was evil in the sight of the LORD like Ahab, whom Jezebel his wife incited. He acted very abominably in going after idols."

Earlier in this chapter, Jezebel had a man, Naboth, killed so that Ahab could take a vineyard - Naboth's family inheritance - for himself.

Are you getting the picture of Ahab's depravity? God's anger was incited against Ahab for his sins. In the next chapter, 1 Kings 22, the prophet Micaiah tells King Ahab that God declared a disaster against him. This happens when Ahab goes into battle against the Syrians. Ahab gets shot with an arrow and bleeds out and dies. Jezebel suffers a more gruesome fate than this in 2 Kings 9.

Why is it helpful to study someone like Ahab with a totally absent fear of God? Because it is the reality of many people in our world today.

A vast majority of people around us have no fear of God and live according to their sinful desires. They are on a path to destruction. God in his justice will not permit them to get away with their actions. To quote Jerry Bridges, "God's wrath has been defined as His settled determination to punish sin. It is more than that; it's a determination to punish sin with a vengeance."[17] One thing that we who desire to fear God can do is to share the truth about God with those who are under God's wrath:

God exists, and he sees everything we do and think. God must punish our sin because he is righteous and just. Because God is loving he offered himself to us as the man Jesus Christ. Jesus bore all the wrath of God that we deserve when he died on the cross. He then defeated death forever by coming back to life. We all must make a decision to trust in Jesus' atoning sacrifice for our salvation and obey him as Lord, or refuse this gift that God offers us and choose to bear the wrath of God on ourselves. This is the message that people like Ahab who don't fear God need to hear. Perhaps God will soften their hard hearts and cause them to repent.

* * *

I hope this chapter has given you a broader understanding of how fearing God plays out. The fear of God may be healthy or unhealthy; a fear of his greatness or a fear of his chastisement. I hope that by looking at examples of these fears we have a deeper knowledge of our own heart posture toward God. Ultimately, we should strive and pray for a healthy fear of God as defined at the beginning of the chapter.

As we continue to discover more of this biblical and beautiful fear of God, I urge you to answer this question for yourself: Do my thoughts and actions demonstrate that I have a healthy fear of the Lord? I hope you ponder this question before journeying through the next chapters and pages.

4

Awesome God

Have you ever visited Rocky Mountain National Park? I've had the pleasure of touring the Rockies in Colorado a few times, and each visit is just as wonderful as the last. Between the breathtaking mountain ranges, the luscious forests, the gentle rivers and streams, the clean cool air, and the plentiful wildlife; there is always something about the experience that both inspires and terrifies me. As I witness the greatness and beauty of the mountains, my mindset is summed up in one word: Awe.

For most people, one of the most common thoughts related to fearing God is being in awe of him. This is a fear of God's greatness. The goal of this chapter is to dive into the awesomeness of God; to feel the rush of God's wonder in a more exhilarating way. I believe that having a feeling of awe for God is one of the essential elements to fearing him in a biblical and beautiful manner.

The word "awesome" as an adjective is often diluted in its meaning. If we are being honest, in our everyday language, we ascribe awe to almost everything: "That touchdown was awesome!" "This restaurant is awesome." "Wasn't that movie awesome?" And with statements such as these we lose touch with what really inspires awe. Many of the things we talk about as being awesome are indeed fun, or interesting, or cool, but they lack the scope or magnitude of why we ascribe that word to God.

If you open up your Bible and read for 60 seconds, you'll quickly begin to realize that God is awesome. The Bible is filled - front to back- with the character of God, so I would encourage you to do your own study of Scripture. For the sake of this chapter, I have selected several passages intended to cultivate our awe.

If God's Word makes it so clear that we are to be in awe of God, what exactly is it about God that inspires this awe? *God's holiness, creation, power, and deeds are what cause us to be in fearful awe of God.* God is awesome because God is holy. There is no one like him. God is awesome because of his creation. He sustains nature and has dominion over it. God is awesome because of his power. He is mighty and unstoppable. God is awesome because of his deeds. He works wonders for his glory and for his chosen people throughout the ages. Many of these "awe factors" are intertwined. For example, God's power and his creation are intertwined, as well as the fact that his deeds show his power and are often seen through creation. Nevertheless, examining them each in turn reveals a holistic view of the awesome God that he is.

God's Holiness

> To whom then will you compare me, that I should be like him? says the Holy One. (Isaiah 40:25)

God is awesome because God is holy, and he thus deserves our fear. For God to be holy means that he is set apart, separate, and distinct from all else. Isaiah 40:25 makes this point with a rhetorical question, "To whom then will you compare me...?" because by definition, nothing can be compared to God. Indeed this holiness is something which finite beings cannot grasp. Theologian A.W. Tozer writes the following:

> We cannot grasp the true meaning of the divine holiness by thinking of someone or something very pure and then raising the concept to the highest degree we are capable of. God's holiness is not simply the best we know infinitely bettered. We know nothing like the divine holiness. It stands apart, unique, unapproachable, incomprehensible, and unattainable. The natural man is blind to it. He may fear God's power and admire His wisdom, but His holiness he cannot even imagine.[18]

While God's holiness is unsearchable and unknowable, God has lovingly given us some insight into his holiness through his Word. According to Scripture, God is set apart from all else because of 1) his moral purity and 2) his self-sufficiency. No other being is morally pure or righteous in and of themselves.

God not only defines what is right and good, but out of him flows all that is right and good. In addition, every being outside of God has to be sustained by God. Our strength to rise up in the morning is borrowed strength. We are dependent, and God is independent. Moral purity and self-sufficiency are the two halves of the pie of God's holiness.

The contrast in moral purity between us and God is infinite. Romans 3 says in verse 10, "None is righteous, no, not one" (and in verse 18 it says that one of the causes of unrighteousness is not fearing God). Later in verse 23 are the famous words, "for all have sinned and fall short of the glory of God." According to these verses from Romans, humans are not morally pure. But if we are being honest, we didn't need Romans to tell us. All we have to do is look at our families or turn on the news. When a child is young, they don't have to be taught to be a bad kid. They have to be taught *not* to lie, *not* to hit other kids, and *not* to steal from the cookie jar. On a larger scale, we see wars and injustice and oppression and pride. This is not foreign to our nature. From the beginning of human history, this is what naturally flows from each person's character. It is not so with God. In a song to God, King David declares, "For you are not a God who delights in wickedness; evil may not dwell with you" (Psalm 5:4). This bent toward evil and delighting in wickedness resides within me, and it resides within you; but no evil or wickedness can be attributed to God. To the contrary, God delights in righteousness; and good dwells with him. It is this moral purity that sets God apart and makes him holy.

God is also holy in the sense that he is self-sufficient. Not only is God sufficient within himself, but he also sustains all of his creation. God exists outside of time and therefore is not bound by it. Unlike us humans, stuck inside the third dimension, God has no such constraint. The God of the Bible is the ultimate reality, the ultimate person, and the ultimate life.

The Bible reinforces this concept of self-sufficiency again and again. In Exodus, God refers to himself as "I AM WHO I AM" (3:14). Before you were born, God is. After you die, God is. Although nations and kingdoms rise and fall, God is. No human is immortal. Last I checked, our mortality rate as a species is 100%, yet God "alone has immortality, who dwells in unapproachable light, whom no one has ever seen or can see" (1 Timothy 6:16). In Revelation 22:13, Jesus says, "I am the Alpha and the Omega, the first and the last, the beginning and the end." No one comes before God and no one comes after God. Scripture attributes this divine quality to Jesus, emphasizing the truth that he is God. In Hebrews 1:3, we read that Jesus "is the radiance of the glory of God and the exact imprint of his nature, and he upholds the universe by the word of his power." And from Acts, "he himself gives to all mankind life and breath and everything" (Acts 17:25). From the billions of massive stars in the universe, to your very breath and heartbeat - it is all constantly sustained by Jesus the divine Son of God. The God of the Bible is self-sufficient, and his self-sufficiency sets him apart and declares his holiness.

Any discussion of God's holiness would be incomplete without mention of his glory. If I were to attempt to define the glory of God, it would be something like this: The glory of God means that 1) His triune holiness and goodness are manifested as perfect radiant beauty, 2) His fame and kingdom increase throughout the world, and 3) He is worshiped in word and deed by men and by angels. There are an ample amount of stories and statements in the Bible that inform this definition. Many of them, like the passages we will look at, showcase God's glory with extreme clarity.

In John 17, Jesus is praying to the Father just hours before submitting himself to a horrific death on a cross and the even more horrific spiritual weight of humanity's sins. In preparation, Jesus prays "Father, the hour has come; glorify your Son that the Son may glorify you... now, Father, glorify me in your own presence with the glory that I had with you before the world existed" (verses 1 and 5). We also read in the chapter before that Jesus shares this knowledge with his disciples: "He [the Holy Spirit] will glorify me, for he will take what is mine and declare it to you" (John 16:14). What this means is that outside of our existence, God is still glorifying himself within the distinct persons of the Godhead. Even outside of our universe existing, God still gets the glory.

In Exodus chapter 33, God asks Moses to lead the encampment of Israelites away from Mount Sinai and into the promised land. At this moment, Moses isn't convinced that God will go with them, so he asks for a sign of God's favor. "Please show me your glory" Moses requests in verse 18. Then in verse 19-23, God describes how he will show his glory to Moses:

> And he said, "I will make all my goodness pass before you and will proclaim before you my name 'The LORD.' And I will be gracious to whom I will be gracious, and will show mercy on whom I will show mercy. But," he said, "you cannot see my face, for man shall not see me and live." And the LORD said, "Behold, there is a place by me where you shall stand on the rock, and while my glory passes by I will put you in a cleft of the rock, and I will cover you with my hand until I have passed by. Then I will take away my

hand, and you shall see my back, but my face shall not be seen." (Exodus 33:19-23)

We learn in the next chapter (Exodus 34) that when God's glory and presence passed by Moses, even though Moses's face was hidden, his skin was left radiant and shining. This brightness was so extravagant that Moses then had to wear a veil when he was around other Israelites. Moses had only seen a minute portion of the glory of God, and yet it had caused his face to radiate. This depiction of God's glory reminds me of Psalm 50:2 which reads, "Out of Zion, the perfection of beauty, God shines forth."

Finally, let us turn our attention to Isaiah's vision of God's glory. Isaiah 6:1-7 is perhaps one of the most profound and intriguing passages of Scripture:

> In the year that King Uzziah died I saw the Lord sitting upon a throne, high and lifted up; and the train of his robe filled the temple. Above him stood the seraphim. Each had six wings: with two he covered his face, and with two he covered his feet, and with two he flew. And one called to another and said:
> "Holy, holy, holy is the LORD of hosts;
> the whole earth is full of his glory!"
> And the foundations of the thresholds shook at the voice of him who called, and the house was filled with smoke. And I said: "Woe is me! For I am lost; for I am a man of unclean lips, and I dwell in the midst of a people of unclean lips; for my eyes have seen the King, the LORD of hosts!"
> Then one of the seraphim flew to me, having in

> his hand a burning coal that he had taken with tongs from the altar. And he touched my mouth and said: "Behold, this has touched your lips; your guilt is taken away, and your sin atoned for."
> (Isaiah 6:1-7)

What would you do if you were in Isaiah's shoes? I'll wager you'd have the exact same reaction as he did. I would too! Your thought process in a matter of milliseconds would go something like this: "I've seen the glory of God, and I deserve to die." The seraphim have a slightly different response to the glory of God. These incredible spiritual beings can't help but praise the Lord and declare his holiness and glory. In Revelation 4:8, a similar refrain is declared day and night around the throne of God by other angelic beings: "Holy, holy, holy, is the Lord God Almighty, who was and is and is to come!" These heavenly hosts are singing and declaring the glory of God. In a similar way, we also should aspire to declare God's glory, not only through song, but in our everyday lives through obedience to him: "So, whether you eat or drink, or whatever you do, do all to the glory of God" (1 Corinthians 10:31).

To reiterate this section: The holiness of God is one of the factors which leaves us in awe and causes us to fear him. To be holy means to be separate, distinct, and set apart. God is set apart from all else because of his moral purity and his self-sufficiency. God receives the glory for his holiness as he is worshiped in perfect splendor for all of eternity.

But wait, there's more.

If you have believed in the name of Jesus; if you are a follower of Christ - saved by the grace of God through faith in his Son - then I have news for you: God is inviting you into his holiness.

He longs for you to have a life of moral purity that reflects his own. 1 Peter 1:15-16 declares, "but as he who called you is holy, you also be holy in all your conduct, since it is written, 'You shall be holy, for I am holy.' " Furthermore, in 1 Peter 2 it tells us that God's people are a "holy nation" (verse 9).

So as we depart from this pivotal discussion on the holiness of God, here is my plea: Don't walk away unchanged. Step into the holiness of God that he has bestowed upon you. Like Moses who was made radiant, or like Isaiah who was made clean, you have been made holy by God. Let that inspire awe and fear in your heart as you behold him. May the following Scripture encourage us as we seek to honor God as holy:

> But the LORD of hosts, him you shall honor as holy.
> Let him be your fear, and let him be your dread.
> (Isaiah 8:13)

God's Creation

On Christmas Eve, 1968; Frank Borman, Bill Anders, and James Lovell were making history. These three astronauts were piloting the Apollo 8 spacecraft in a mission to orbit around the moon and return to earth. They were the first humans to ever see the dark side of the moon, and the first to see the earth rise in the sky from another world. On this day, as they entered lunar orbit, they sent a transmission back to Earth which was broadcast live to millions of people worldwide.[19] Here is what they said:

We are now approaching lunar sunrise, and for all the people back on Earth, the crew of Apollo 8 has a message that we would like to send to you.

In the beginning God created the heaven and the earth. And the earth was without form, and void; and darkness was upon the face of the deep. And the Spirit of God moved upon the face of the waters. And God said, Let there be light: and there was light. And God saw the light, that it was good: and God divided the light from the darkness. And God called the light Day, and the darkness he called Night. And the evening and the morning were the first day. And God said, Let there be a firmament in the midst of the waters, and let it divide the waters from the waters. And God made the firmament, and divided the waters which were under the firmament from the waters which were above the firmament: and it was so. And God called the firmament Heaven. And the evening and the morning were the second day. And God said, Let the waters under the heaven be gathered together unto one place, and let the dry land appear: and it was so. And God called the dry land Earth; and the gathering together of the waters called the Seas: and God saw that it was good.

And from the crew of Apollo 8, we close with good night, good luck, a Merry Christmas - and God bless all of you, all of you on the good Earth.[20]

I think it's so cool that - while in space - these astronauts quoted the creation account from Genesis 1! From this voyage there is a photograph taken by Bill Anders called *Earthrise*. It is worth a quick Google search! In light of their vantage point, the astronauts wanted to remind their listeners that God made everything good.

This story always gives me chills. It gives me chills because of the magnificence of God's creation. It wasn't just God's creation the astronauts were beholding from the window of Apollo 8. They were also witnessing the reality that God's creation is good. In Genesis 1, it notes how God saw that his creation "was good" six times, and then when God had finished, "it was very good" (Genesis 1:31).

That was before the fall of man, yet God's goodness is still observable. Even with the pollution and fallout that our sin has introduced into creation, God still hasn't abandoned what is his masterpiece, and we can still see his goodness. From Psalm 50 he proclaims, "For every beast of the forest is mine" (verse 10) and "all that moves in the field is mine" (verse 11) and "the world and its fullness are mine" (verse 12).

The truth of the matter is that God's creation is good because it points to who he is. When we see beauty in creation; we can hear it declaring God's praises and glory. As image bearers of God, we are hardwired to recognize his goodness around us. We can't look upon a newborn infant, or a seashore at sunset, or a grand mountain range, or a starlit sky without having a feeling inside of us that says, "This is awesome." That is the goodness of God displayed in creation. This goodness in creation inspires awe in us toward the Creator. The following verses leave no room for doubt that creation speaks to who God is:

> For his invisible attributes, namely, his eternal power

and divine nature, have been clearly perceived, ever since the creation of the world, in the things that have been made. (Romans 1:20a)

The heavens declare the glory of God, and the sky above proclaims his handiwork. Day to day pours out speech, and night to night reveals knowledge. (Psalm 19:1-2)

If you want to be in awe of God because of his attributes revealed in creation, go hiking on a nature trail, or take a weekend to camp out in nature, or gaze out the window next time you're on a flight. Turn off your phone and pray while you're out in nature. Creation is always speaking, and it says that God is good and that God is awesome. Yet, with all of this wonderful handiwork that you can observe, there is one creation that God has crafted even more beautifully: You. As a human, you are made in the image of God, and you are therefore God's most sacred creation:

For you formed my inward parts; you knitted me together in my mother's womb. I praise you, for I am fearfully and wonderfully made. Wonderful are your works; my soul knows it very well. My frame was not hidden from you, when I was being made in secret, intricately woven in the depths of the earth. Your eyes saw my unformed substance; in your book were written, every one of them, the days that were formed for me, when as yet there was none of them. (Psalm 139:13-16)

It was not mere biology that formed you, it was the proactive sovereignty of God. What we see in these verses is that you are not a mistake, but rather a masterpiece. Because God has marvelously crafted you, he knows every day of your life, every tear that you cry, and every aspect of your personality. Most importantly, God made you to not be satisfied with anything other than reflecting his image and knowing him.

To conclude this section, God's creation is awesome because he created it to be beautiful and good. As image bearers of God, we are hardwired to recognize God's goodness revealed in nature. From the corners of the universe, to the cells inside your body; all of creation reveals God's glory.

Most importantly, God designed you to be the pinnacle of his creation that reflects him most closely. He knows you, and desires you to know your Maker. As we marvel in awe over God's creation, let it inspire awe and fear of him. Let our hearts echo the words of Jonah the prophet: "I fear the LORD, the God of heaven, who made the sea and the dry land" (Jonah 1:9).

God's Power

In observing God's holiness and creation, we have inadvertently begun to unearth his power. By God's own strength he is sufficient and set apart, and by his own might he created and sustains all things. A fitting example from Scripture that conveys this power is in Job 38, where God appears to the man Job, and rebukes Job's protest that he is in the right and God is in the wrong. To answer Job, God addresses him with a series of rhetorical questions which display God's sovereign power over the unseen forces of nature. It is an excellent chapter for meditating on the power of God as it relates to his holiness and creation. In addition to these important aspects of the power of God, I want us to lean in to another attribute of God that proclaims his power: his love.

The topic of God's love is vast and quite honestly unfathomable, so our study of how it relates to his power will be brief. Yet, it is my hope that this discussion on an immeasurable love will generate a sense of awe and fear of our all-powerful Lover. So I begin with a question: What better example of the limitless power of God's love than Jesus Christ, the Son of God, who loved us unto death? John Bunyan once wrote that in order to grow in the grace of fearing God, you must take a "proper look at Christ, hanging on the cross for your sins."[21] What Jesus did on the cross demonstrates his power and his love. Behold the strength of God's love:

> For I am sure that neither death nor life, nor angels nor rulers, nor things present nor things to come, nor powers, nor height nor depth, nor anything else in all creation, will be able to separate us from the love of God in Christ Jesus our Lord.
> (Romans 8:38-39)

If God's love for us in Christ is that powerful, then there is nothing that can stand in its way. As a Christ-follower, the power of God's love for you in Christ Jesus transcends all other powers. What about demonic oppression? Jesus' love is more powerful. What about our own shame, regret, and past mistakes? Jesus' love is more powerful. What about the combined power of the human race and all spiritual forces at any given time? Jesus' love is still more powerful.

When I was a teenager I was ashamed of my sin and felt certain that I had out-sinned God's love. This drove me away from God, and caused me to fear God in a sinful way. It was clearly unhealthy. However, when I finally believed the truth from Romans 8 that nothing - not even myself - could separate me from God's all-powerful love, it ignited a spark of awe, joy, and hope within me. This truth pulled me out of improper and unhealthy fear of God into a biblical and beautiful fear of God.

Jesus himself said in John 10:28-29, "I give them eternal life, and they will never perish, and no one will snatch them out of my hand. My Father, who has given them to me, is greater than all, and no one is able to snatch them out of the Father's hand." Not only will God the Son never let you go, but God the Father will never let you go. Whatever or whoever is condemning you today is helpless to loose the grip of God's embrace. If God has given you eternal life and the promise of his presence, there is no force that can nullify it.

The resurrection of Jesus proves the power of God's love. The Bible teaches that "If the Spirit of him who raised Jesus from the dead dwells in you, he who raised Christ Jesus from the dead will also give life to your mortal bodies through his Spirit who dwells in you." (Romans 8:11), and "God raised the Lord and will also raise us up by his power" (1 Corinthians 6:14). The power of God the Spirit not only raised Jesus from the dead, but it also regenerates us, and raises us up into eternal life. Why did he do this? Why would God use his power to grant us the life of Christ on earth and eternal life in heaven? What would cause him to make us alive again? Ephesians gives us the answer:

> But God, being rich in mercy, because of the great love with which he loved us, even when we were dead in our trespasses, made us alive together with Christ—

> by grace you have been saved (Ephesians 2:4-5)

Fellow Christian, because of God's great mercy toward you, he resurrected you. Your own contributions and merit have no bearing on your spiritual rejuvenation. By God's power, he brought you from spiritual death to spiritual life. All the achievements of human science combined cannot defy physical death, much less spiritual death. But the love of God overcomes.

The love of God puts his power on full display. No force can pull you from the love of Jesus. No strength can tear you from the arms of the Father. No authority can stop the Spirit of God from sealing you for eternal life. God's power is unyielding, and it is intertwined with his love. Coming to grips with these truths should beget awe in our thoughts toward him. I close this section with a Psalm:

> Once God has spoken; twice have I heard this: that power belongs to God, and that to you, O Lord, belongs steadfast love. (Psalm 62:11-12a)

God's Deeds

Every display of God's power - each thing he creates and each manifestation of his glory - is a showcase for the awesome deeds of the Lord. These deeds of God, which have occurred throughout all history, are also referred to as his "wonders" or his "works" in the pages of Scripture. None of these deeds are isolated. God is always at work developing his grand story. It is a story of his own love, justice, and righteousness, and the finale is God's ultimate glorification and triumph. Whether we opt to follow God or not, we still play a part in that story.

Yet God has graciously invited us to join him in his story; to flip through the pages and see where he is working in our lives, around the world, and throughout history.

If you have an ESV Bible, the heading above Psalm 66 will read "How Awesome are Your Deeds". The content of this Psalm drives the point home:

> Say to God, "How awesome are your deeds! So great is your power that your enemies come cringing to you. (Psalm 66:3)

> Come and see what God has done: he is awesome in his deeds toward the children of man. (Psalm 66:5)

> Come and hear, all you who fear God, and I will tell what he has done for my soul. (Psalm 66:16)

How awesome are God's deeds! In this Psalm, we are invited to both *hear* and *see* the works of the Lord. In other words, we are invited to experience all that he has done. This chapter mentions two specific deeds that God has accomplished, and they are worth discussing.

Verse 6 declares, "He turned the sea into dry land; they passed through the river on foot." This is a callback to the Exodus of the Hebrews out of the land of Egypt. The deliverance of God's people out of Egypt is an awesome work of the Lord. The first 15 chapters of Exodus are dedicated to this account. When I was younger, I saw a movie that is still one of my favorites to this day: *The Prince of Egypt* [22]. It tells the story of Moses and of God's deliverance. Each time I see this masterful film, I am amazed and inspired by how God worked deliverance for the

Hebrews! I highly recommend watching this film if you haven't, because it highlights one of the most significant deeds of God in the Old Testament.

Verse 16 says, "I will tell what he has done for my soul." This is the second deed of God mentioned in Psalm 66, and it is more personal. What has God done for the Psalmist's soul? We see the answer in verse 19: "But truly God has listened; he has attended to the voice of my prayer." This beckons us to evaluate ourselves in the same way that the Psalmist did: What great things has God done for you (See 1 Samuel 12:24)? Have you declared to others the story of how God delivered you (See Psalm 40:9-10)? If we honestly examine our lives, we may be surprised at the number of things we have to be grateful to God for. He has done countless things for us that we don't deserve. Have you ever thought about where you might be right now if God had not intervened in your life? Would you be alone? In jail? An addict? Anxious or depressed? Spiritually dead? Ponder this for a moment. Allow yourself to be awestruck by the wonders of God in your own life.

Perhaps you are being faced by one or more of these devastating situations. Maybe you are questioning if God will really come through for you? Take comfort from the Psalmist's experience, "Truly God has listened." God is not deaf. He is not powerless, and in Christ you cannot be separated from his love. Cling to his promises knowing that one day you will be able to say with the Psalmist, "I will tell what he has done for my soul."

We now turn to God's deeds in the New Testament. At the time of writing this, I am in the process of studying through the book of Acts. It documents the birth of the Christian Church and the lives of the disciples and apostles after Jesus resurrected and ascended to heaven. Traditionally, the full name of Acts is "The Acts of the Apostles", yet, as I have been studying through this book, I can't help but realize it is truly about the acts of God. Acts is an excellent case study into the awesome nature of God's deeds, and how he invites his followers into them.

The most awesome and quintessential work that God did for us was sending us his Son Jesus. Philippians 2:6-11 describes this wondrous work of the Son of God, "who, though he was in the form of God, did not count equality with God a thing to be grasped, but emptied himself, by taking the form of a servant, being born in the likeness of men. And being found in human form, he humbled himself by becoming obedient to the point of death, even death on a cross. Therefore God has highly exalted him and bestowed on him the name that is above every name, so that at the name of Jesus every knee should bow, in heaven and on earth and under the earth, and every tongue confess that Jesus Christ is Lord, to the glory of God the Father."

This is the ultimate work of God. It is the climax of his story. The sacrifice and exaltation of Jesus, and the subsequent glorification of the Father is no doubt God's most awesome deed to consider.

* * *

Being in awe of God is vital and necessary to having a proper fear of God. This is a fear of God's greatness, and it is indispensable to a healthy fear of the Lord. God is awesome because of his holiness, creation, power, and deeds. Gaining a holistic view of all of these awe factors will compel us to have a more biblical and beautiful fear of him.

5

God's Judgment

In the last chapter we covered the topic of being in awe of God. This is a fear of God's greatness. In this chapter, I want to discuss an important part of fearing God's chastisement, that is, the fear of God's judgment. This aspect of fearing God's chastisement stems from the knowledge that God is dangerous to those who oppose him. Back in the first chapter, one of our definitions of fear was having an unpleasant emotion caused from an awareness of danger. This fear is generally tied with the idea that God will judge sinners and pour out his wrath on them.

The fear of God's judgment can be acted upon in both healthy and unhealthy ways. In an unhealthy fashion, people respond either by neglecting God's love and mercy, or by downplaying his justice. Conversely, if you have a healthy understanding of the danger involved in God's judgment, your heart will be drawn toward gratitude for the grace that God offers, causing you to walk more closely with him. A right understanding of God's judgment is what I seek to showcase in this chapter, so as to produce a proper fear of him in our hearts.

If you are not a Christian, I hope that you will read and digest this chapter with humility and pondering, and that it will awaken a desire in you to become an object of God's infinite love and mercy, rather than an object of God's infinite judgment and wrath.

If you are a Christian, you may be tempted to skip this chapter, or to zone out and not meditate on this topic as much. You may think to yourself, "I am no longer under God's judgment. It was poured out on his Son on my behalf, and I have trusted in him. I have been saved by faith in Jesus. I am now under grace, I am justified before God, and I may commune with God, both now and in eternity." This is absolutely true. One hundred percent. However, if your next thought is something like, "Because I am no longer under God's wrath, I don't need to wrestle with this uncomfortable subject," then I would urge you to reconsider.

There are two reasons why the topic of fearing God's judgment is important to followers of Jesus. First, Jesus says so: "I tell you, my friends, do not fear those who kill the body, and after that have nothing more that they can do. But I will warn you whom to fear: fear him who, after he has killed, has authority to cast into hell. Yes, I tell you, fear him!" (Luke 12:4-5). A similar teaching from Jesus is found in Matthew 10:28. The significance is that in both cases, if we look at the surrounding context, we see Jesus is *exclusively* saying these things to his disciples.

Jesus' disciples were his students. These were the apprentices of Jesus who would go on to start the early church; most of whom would die for their faith. Consequently, for followers of Jesus today, we should understand that Jesus wants us to know the severity of God's judgment, and to fear him because of it. God alone can cast people into hell, and God alone can "destroy the soul" (Matthew 10:28). As modern day disciples of Jesus, we would do well to acknowledge this.

Aside from Jesus' command, why else should believers consider God's judgment? We should never forget the Good News of Jesus, and we should never forget who we were before Christ intervened in our lives. In order for the Good News to be good news, we must understand the bad news.

The bad news is our sin. Because of our wickedness, God, who is holy and righteous, must judge us and pour out his wrath on us. The good news is Jesus' sacrificial atonement on the cross in our place. Jesus took God's wrath for us. We will never get promoted out of this fundamental truth; and we will always need to be reminded of it. Thus we should daily consider the ever-present Gospel that saves us. One of the most iconic passages that describes the Gospel is Ephesians 2:1-10. It is well worth an individual study. There is no greater truth to ponder and it all starts with an understanding of the judgment of God.

Judgment of the Wicked

Now that we understand the need for this topic if we are to have healthy fear, let us consider the why: Why does God judge? In short, God judges us because he is good, he alone has the authority, he alone is holy; and he delights in justice and righteousness. Two things must be made clear:

1. People are evil. There is no good in us. We all sin, are wicked to the core, and reject God. We do this not only in our actions, but in our thoughts. We are guilty.
2. God is good. Because he defines what is good, that makes him the judge of what is right and wrong. A good judge

must punish the guilty.

There are some who will say that because God is loving, he does not judge. They perceive God's judgment as unloving. The problem with this idea is that it fails to factor in what God has done out of love to keep us all from experiencing eternal judgment. God the Father poured out his wrath on Jesus, the Son of God, who took upon himself the visible and invisible sins of every person for all time. He did this to make a way for us to know him and have eternal life. This is how much God loves us. For God to judge does not mean that his love is absent. Scripture itself teaches us that God is the judge:

> For God will bring every deed into judgment, with every secret thing, whether good or evil. (Ecclesiastes 12:14)

> The LORD is a jealous and avenging God; the LORD is avenging and wrathful; the LORD takes vengeance on his adversaries and keeps wrath for his enemies. The LORD is slow to anger and great in power, and the LORD will by no means clear the guilty. (Nahum 1:2-3a)

> For the wrath of God is revealed from heaven against all ungodliness and unrighteousness of men, who by their unrighteousness suppress the truth.
> (Romans 1:18)

> Do you suppose, O man—you who judge those who practice such things and yet do them yourself—that

> you will escape the judgment of God? Or do you presume on the riches of his kindness and forbearance and patience, not knowing that God's kindness is meant to lead you to repentance? But because of your hard and impenitent heart you are storing up wrath for yourself on the day of wrath when God's righteous judgment will be revealed. (Romans 2:3-5)

The biblical narrative gives us good insight to the "why" behind God's judgment - our own sin. Once accused of our own sin, we cannot post bail ourselves, and we cannot be exonerated on our own. Even if we try to make our own case for our own perceived good deeds, they are tarnished by our evil hearts and our pride, and condemn us all the more. The Bible says in Jeremiah 17:9 that "the heart is deceitful above all things, and desperately sick." We are all corrupt and choose to fall away from God. In fact, not only are we all corrupt, but we all are prone to abominable deeds. This is not only true of some people, this is true of all people for all time:

> The fool says in his heart, "There is no God." They are corrupt, they do abominable deeds; there is none who does good. The LORD looks down from heaven on the children of man, to see if there are any who understand, who seek after God. They have all turned aside; together they have become corrupt; there is none who does good, not even one. (Psalm 14:1-3)

I am reminded of the popular verse Romans 3:23: "for all have sinned and fall short of the glory of God." After you've sinned once, it is enough to keep you from God's glory and earn you eternal death, because you have offended the eternal God. Consider Adam and Eve: They sinned once, and not only were they banished from God's presence, but their actions introduced into creation the fallout of sin and corruption. That is the weight of each sin you and I commit. R.C. Sproul writes, "What was the penalty for sin in the original created order? 'The soul who sins is the one who will die' (Ezekiel 18:4). In creation all sin is deemed worthy of death. Every sin is a capital offense."[23]

Although God's judgment for all sin, wickedness, and evil is an eternal judgment; we may also experience God's judgment on this side of eternity. Throughout the Bible there are many stories of nations and individuals who are punished severely for their sin. We need not look far: One example is King Nebuchadnezzar of Babylon, who ascribed glory, power, and majesty to himself instead of God, so God immediately intervened. King Nebuchadnezzar "was driven from among men and ate grass like an ox, and his body was wet with the dew of heaven till his hair grew as long as eagles' feathers, and his nails were like birds' claws" (Daniel 4:33).

We know based on Scripture that earthly judgments are certain. It says in Romans 2:9 that, "there will be tribulation and distress for every human being who does evil," and Psalm 73:18-19 says of the wicked, "Truly you [God] set them in slippery places; you make them fall to ruin. How they are destroyed in a moment, swept away utterly by terrors!" Thus, God will not only bring eternal wrath upon the ungodly, but also immediate consequences. This should increase our fear of God in a way that leads to repentance and obedience.

Judgment of Believers

Christians do not escape judgment. If you are a follower of Christ, rest assured you will not receive the wrath due your sins. You have trusted in Jesus; upon whom the wrath of the Father was poured out on your behalf. However, you still fall under the discipline of your Father. We will cover the topic of God's discipline in chapter 8.

There are two places in Scripture that are crystal clear on judgment of believers. We will briefly examine each one to paint a clearer picture. The first is below:

> For we must all appear before the judgment seat of Christ, so that each one may receive what is due for what he has done in the body, whether good or evil.
> (2 Corinthians 5:10)

This statement is written by Paul, and the surrounding context is a conversation about how we Christians eagerly await our heavenly dwelling with God. We are to take courage and have faith, because God has promised us heaven through the Holy Spirit. It is in *this* context that Paul inserts, "we must all appear before the judgment seat of Christ." Not only that, but we are to receive rewards from Christ for what we did on earth. In the first letter to the Corinthians, Paul actually gives greater context for this judgment on believers:

> Each one's work will become manifest, for the Day will disclose it, because it will be revealed by fire, and the fire will test what sort of work each one has done. If the work that anyone has built on the foundation

survives, he will receive a reward. If anyone's work is burned up, he will suffer loss, though he himself will be saved, but only as through fire.
(1 Corinthians 3:13-15)

On this Day of the Lord, at the end of time, each of us will have our lives examined and scrutinized by the holy fire of God. This is not to punish us, but to reward us. If we wasted our lives, and allowed the passions of the old self to flare up, then we did not complete what was prepared for us to accomplish for the glory of God. These are the "good works, which God prepared beforehand, that we should walk in them" (Ephesians 2:10). We were saved by God's grace and welcomed into God's kingdom, but we allowed comfort, entertainment, money, apathy, or culture to dictate our lives instead of God's commands. For this our reward is nothing. Christ tells us to "lay up for yourselves treasures in heaven" (Matthew 6:20). There are eternal rewards on the table for us if we live our lives to the glory of God in Christ Jesus. At the end of my life, I desire to hear the words "Well done, good and faithful servant" (Matthew 25:21). My life will be judged, just like every other follower of Christ.

There is one more judgment passage written to believers, and it should cause us to deeply examine ourselves. This judgment comes from the book of Hebrews:

For if we go on sinning deliberately after receiving the knowledge of the truth, there no longer remains a sacrifice for sins, but a fearful expectation of judgment, and a fury of fire that will consume the adversaries. Anyone who has set aside the law of Moses dies without mercy on the evidence of two or three witnesses. How much worse punishment, do you think, will be deserved by the one who has trampled underfoot the Son of God, and has profaned the blood of the covenant by which he was sanctified, and has outraged the Spirit of grace? For we know him who said, 'Vengeance is mine; I will repay.' And again, 'The Lord will judge his people.' It is a fearful thing to fall into the hands of the living God.

(Hebrews 10:26-31)

If you do any research on this passage, you will find that there is an interpretive disagreement. Some people say that this refers to people who are Christians, and some people say it refers to those who are fake Christians. In the context of the whole book of Hebrews, I believe it probably refers to apostates rather than genuine believers. The message, however, remains relevant to us today. Consider this: Does it matter who these verses are aimed at? Does it really change the truth about this passage? Are not both genuine believers and fake Christians found in the same congregations? So we must examine this solemn warning of God's judgment on those who say they are sanctified and who know the truth, yet continue in a lifestyle of deliberate sin. To say that we trust in Jesus' atoning sacrifice to cover our sin and then embrace a lifestyle of sin disregards and dishonors Christ's blood poured out for us. To be sanctified is to be made holy, and we cannot be people who are sanctified and also deliberately living in sin. This is a contradiction that offends the work of Jesus. This behavior places us in the center of God's crosshair. According to Hebrews, he will judge those who live in this manner. The blood of Jesus is not to be taken lightly.

* * *

With this brief overview of why God judges, and why all people fall under his judgment, we must now examine the subject matter of God's *eternal* judgment and wrath on sinners: the place of hell.

What is hell?

Culturally, the word hell is now used so often that it has lost its weight and severity. You see people use it in expletive phrases such as "that hurt like *hell*" or "what in the *hell*." To take things a step further, this occurs with the word damn. It is used to express states of being frustrated, emotional or even impressed. In its rightful meaning, to be "damned" is to be under God's condemnation and judgment; specifically in hell. This tells me that people in this day and age do not take God's judgment seriously.

Our society has moved so far from God that to acknowledge hell as real will immediately place you on the fringes of society. To say that people go to hell is considered hate speech. If you genuinely believe that such a place exists, then you are considered to be out-of-date or delusional. Yet, God's Word is true, and God's Word tells us that hell is real.

So how do we define it? Matt Chandler offers this definition: "Hell, when all is said and done, is the absence of God's goodness and blessedness. Therefore, hell is the absence of anything we can think of that's good, right, comforting, joyous, happy, and peaceful."[24] John Piper has this to say about the word hell as it is used in the Bible: "The word *hell (gehenna)* occurs in the New Testament twelve times—eleven on the lips of Jesus. It is not a myth created by dismal and angry preachers. It is the solemn warning of the Son of God who died to deliver sinners from its curse. We ignore it at great risk."[25]

The reality of hell is indeed a solemn one. At any given moment, you and I are just one step away from eternity. Whether it's a heart attack, a stroke, a car accident, a drive-by shooting, or choking on food; we are prone to forget that we aren't immortal. When we die, we have either accepted the atoning blood of Jesus which satisfies God's wrath and makes us righteous before him, or we have not. If we have not, then we are still in our sin. And that sin earns us a one-way ticket to hell.

Jesus says in John 5:28-29, "Do not marvel at this, for an hour is coming when all who are in the tombs will hear his voice and come out, those who have done good to the resurrection of life, and those who have done evil to the resurrection of judgment." These are the only two options after physical death. We don't fade into nothingness with our conscience ceasing to exist. We aren't reincarnated into another human or animal based on some sort of karma. The reality is that when we die, we become either an object of God's infinite love and mercy or an object of God's infinite wrath. We awake to eternal life in heaven or eternal death in hell.

This is where I want us to slow down for a moment. Below you will see a list of all the different depictions of hell that I was able to find in the Bible. I ask that you would read this list slowly and carefully. All of these truths evaluated together can give us an idea of hell.

In the Bible, hell is defined as:

- Everlasting shame and contempt (Daniel 12:2)

- A fiery furnace where there will be weeping and gnashing of teeth (Matthew 13:42)
- The outer darkness (Matthew 22:13)
- An eternal fire prepared for those cursed by God, along with the devil and his angels (Matthew 25:41)
- Eternal punishment (Matthew 25:46)
- The unquenchable fire (Mark 9:43)
- A place where worms do not die and fire is not quenched (Mark 9:48)
- The abyss (Luke 8:31)
- Hades; A fiery place of torment and anguish (Luke 16:23-24)
- Punishment of eternal destruction, separated from God's presence and glorious might (2 Thessalonians 1:9)
- A place with chains of gloomy darkness (2 Peter 2:4)
- Punishment of eternal fire (Jude 1:7)
- A bottomless pit (Revelation 9:2)
- A place where torment rises like smoke for ever and ever, with no rest, day or night (Revelation 14:11)
- A lake that burns with fire and sulfur (Revelation 19:20)
- The second death (Revelation 21:8)

This is the final destination for those who do not know Jesus. If you don't have a relationship with Jesus, this is the trajectory of your life as well. From this list we can glean that hell is not a joke. Contrary to silly depictions of hell, it isn't a sauna of horned red devils with pitchforks. As described in the Bible, hell is much worse. Hell is torment, hell is isolation, hell is endless, and hell is hopeless.

Hell is torment. Burning is the key word in many of the depictions of hell. There is a reason that people caught in burning buildings would rather jump out and fall than face the flames. Fire is devastating. Our only experience with fire is the fire of earth, but the fires of hell we can only imagine. This is the flame that awaits sinners.

Hell is isolation. Those in hell are ultimately separated and cut off from God. There is no communion or fellowship with him. Studies show that in prisons, solitary confinement leads to decreased memory, negative psychiatric effects, and emotional numbness.[26] I am convinced that the lonesomeness of hell will have a more catastrophic effect.

When God punished Cain, the first murderer, this is how Cain responded: "Cain said to the LORD, 'My punishment is greater than I can bear. Behold, you have driven me today away from the ground, and from your face I shall be hidden. I shall be a fugitive and a wanderer on the earth, and whoever finds me will kill me'" (Genesis 4:13-14). Note the priority of Cain's concern. What frightened Cain the most was not the possibility of being killed, but of being hidden from the face of God. He feared loss of relationship with his Creator. This was where his mind went to first. In that moment Cain's fear was in the right place. Maybe we can learn something from the first murderer.

Hell is endless. Just as God and heaven are eternal, hell is also eternal. This is what Jonathan Edwards once said of hell:

> It is everlasting wrath. It would be dreadful to suffer this fierceness and wrath of Almighty God one moment; but you must suffer it to all eternity. There will be no end to this exquisite horrible misery. When you look forward, you shall see a long for ever, a boundless duration before you, which will swallow

up your thoughts, and amaze your soul; and you will absolutely despair of ever having any deliverance, any end, any mitigation, any rest at all. You will know certainly that you must wear out long ages, millions of millions of ages, in wrestling and conflicting with this almighty merciless vengeance; and then when you have so done, when so many ages have actually been spent by you in this manner, you will know that all is but a point to what remains. So that your punishment will indeed be infinite. Oh, who can express what the state of a soul in such circumstances is![27]

Hell is hopeless. Once someone is there, the Bible says that there is no rescue or remedy from hell. Luke 16:26 speaks of a "great chasm" fixed in place between heaven and hell so that "none may cross" from one side to the other. In hell, hope is extinct.

At this point I want to point out that fearing hell does not lead to true repentance or a change of heart. In Luke 8:31, we see that even demons fear being tormented in hell and yet they are not repentant. Demons do not rule hell. It is not a kingdom of Satan. Demons will suffer the wrath due their treachery as well as those who die in their sin. True repentance comes from looking to God instead of looking to hell.

Yes, knowing about hell is important. However, it is my opinion that scaring people into the church by overemphasizing hell actually does them a disservice. If we focus on primarily fearing hell, then we will lose sight of primarily fearing God. He is the one that sinners have offended.

We must obey Jesus' command: Fear the One who can cast you into hell and destroy your soul. We must remember that each of us has sinned and earned residency in hell, yet God is patient and merciful. He has given us time on earth in order to respond to the Good News of Jesus and be saved. As 2 Peter 3:15 says, "count the patience of our Lord as salvation."

* * *

If you are someone who perceives God's judgment and wrath as unjust or evil, I would challenge you to check your heart. The Psalmist says of God, "With the merciful you show yourself merciful; with the blameless man you show yourself blameless; with the purified you show yourself pure; and with the crooked you make yourself seem tortuous" (Psalms 18:25-26). The Hebrew word for "crooked" here means *perverse, twisted, or deceitful.* If these adjectives describe you, then of course you will have a cynical view of God as tortuous and mean. Of course your heart will be opposed to him.

However, if your heart is pure toward God, and you seek to live a life honoring to him, then your perspective of God changes. You will no longer see God as a tortuous overlord in the sky waiting to send people to a fiery dungeon. He becomes a precious treasure more pure than refined gold. More than that God becomes your friend with death-defying love for you. By his grace, that is who he is to me now.

I take great comfort in knowing that God desires to show mercy, patience and love toward his enemies, rather than judgment. God's heart is for each of us to experience reconciliation with him instead of his wrath. What pleases God is to heal and restore. He has revealed to us as much.

In 2 Peter 3:9, we are told that, "The Lord is not slow to fulfill his promise as some count slowness, but is patient toward you, not wishing that any should perish, but that all should reach repentance." This statement amazes me because of its inclusiveness. God doesn't wish *any* to perish. God knows the thoughts and actions of each person, and he still desires them to turn to him.

This desire of God is consistent throughout all Scripture. His desire to forgive sinners did not begin with the birth of Jesus. In Ezekiel 33:11, the prophet writes, "Say to them, As I live, declares the LORD God, I have no pleasure in the death of the wicked, but that the wicked turn from his way and live; turn back, turn back from your evil ways, for why will you die, O house of Israel?" God desires us to turn away from our sin. Why? Sin always leads to death. Furthermore, Isaiah 28:21 says that judgment is "strange" and "alien" to God. This is not to say that God is more loving and forgiving than he is just. What it does mean is that God can pass over our sins in such a way that it powerfully demonstrates his love and his justice all at once.

Judgment Passed Over

> For the life of the flesh is in the blood, and I have given it for you on the altar to make atonement for your souls, for it is the blood that makes atonement by the life.
> (Leviticus 17:11)

After seeing what the Bible says about hell, you might be squirming in your seat. I get it. These realities are very discomforting and frightening. It all sounds like a waffle cone scoop of bad news. Fortunately, there is a whole carton of good news.

The good news is that God's eternal judgment of your sin can be atoned for through faith in Jesus Christ.

Whether you need a reminder of this truth that you believe, or you are hearing this for the first time, I will say it again: Faith in Jesus Christ frees you from God's eternal judgment.

To understand what this means, let us look at an important story from Scripture which illustrates God's judgment and mercy. Our story is found in Exodus 12. God's people, the Israelites, were slaves in Egypt. They had begged God to free them and he sent Moses to command Pharaoh to let them go. When Pharaoh refused, God struck Egypt with nine devastating plagues because of Pharaoh's disobedience to God. Yet Pharaoh's heart was hardened and he would not free the Israelite slaves. So God persisted in judgment.

The tenth and final plague on the Egyptians, which finally freed the Israelites, was extremely deadly. There was a night quickly approaching where God was going to kill all the firstborn people and firstborn animals in Egypt. God told Moses that in order for the Israelites to be safe from the final plague, each family had to slaughter a spotless lamb, paint their doorposts and lintel with the blood of the lamb, and not leave their homes until the next day. The Israelites did this, and were spared. The death of an innocent lamb provided the covering which turned away God's wrath. Judgment had passed over them, and they were free.

We must also paint our doors with the blood of the lamb. Not the doors of our dorms, houses, or apartments; but the doors of our hearts. God's judgment is coming and it will not pass over us unless we have the blood of the lamb protecting us. Where then is our lamb? Around 2000 years ago, a man named John the Baptist, filled with the Holy Spirit, saw Jesus approaching and exclaimed, "Behold, the Lamb of God, who takes away the sin of the world!" (John 1:29).

Jesus is our Passover lamb. He took our sins upon himself and died in our place. Hanging on the cross, Jesus truly experienced the hell that we deserve. Jesus bore the eternal weight of God's wrath in our place. If we choose to trust in his blood to cover us, and believe that he is the only one who can save us from the wrath of God, then the judgment due our sins passes over us.

Apart from Jesus we are all "children of wrath" and "dead in our trespasses" (Ephesians 2:3,5). Yet Jesus offers us the remedy when he says, "Truly, truly, I say to you, whoever hears my word and believes him who sent me has eternal life. He does not come into judgment, but has passed from death to life" (John 5:24).

God loves us so much that he provides a clean slate to us in the person of Jesus. If we trust in Jesus and embrace his love, then we need not fear eternal judgment. Jesus' beloved disciple John wrote, "By this is love perfected with us, so that we may have confidence for the day of judgment, because as he is so also are we in this world. There is no fear in love, but perfect love casts out fear. For fear has to do with punishment, and whoever fears has not been perfected in love" (1 John 4:17-18).

Do you fear the punishment of God? Embrace his love extended to you through Jesus. Jesus is the mediator and arbiter for your sins. He alone stands between you and eternal judgment... if you let him. Before Jesus came to Earth, the man Job proclaimed this of God:

> For he is not a man, as I am, that I might answer him,
> that we should come to trial together. There is no

> arbiter between us, who might lay his hand on us both. Let him take his rod away from me, and let not dread of him terrify me. Then I would speak without fear of him, for I am not so in myself. (Job 9:32-35)

Job was terribly afraid to approach God because of his sin. Job yearned for someone who could lay their hands on the shoulder of both God and Job and plead Job's case. For us living on this side of the cross, we know who Job was hoping for: "For there is one God, and there is one mediator between God and men, the man Christ Jesus" (1 Timothy 2:5).

If you have not trusted in Christ Jesus as your Savior and chosen to obey him as your Lord, today is the day. Tomorrow could be too late. You will face God one day, and the eternal wrath due your sin will either fall on you, or it will be passed over by the blood that Jesus shed on the cross. Don't try to represent yourself in the courts of heaven. Cry out to Jesus today.

A Right Response

> Rescue those who are being taken away to death;
> hold back those who are stumbling to the slaughter.
> (Proverbs 24:11)

If you do not consider yourself a follower of Jesus, then I hope you will not harden your heart. Choose to fear God and draw near to him. Fearing God's judgment can lead you in two directions: either hatred of God or love of God. Michael Reeves explains that, "Sinful fear is not merely a matter of sinful actions: it *hates* God, despising him as a revenging Judge, and *therefore* acts sinfully. In contrast, a right fear *loves* God, cherishing him as a holy Father, and therefore has a sincere longing to be like him."[28] It is my prayer that you would choose right and healthy fear, and that you would love God and trust him with your life.

If you are someone who has already placed your faith in Jesus, then I hope that you will also choose a path of healthy fear. Fear God by having love and compassion for the lost people around you. Let them know that they are sinners in need of a Savior. For us who are saved, a healthy fear of God's judgment means that we fear God on behalf of the unbeliever who may not fear God. Consider the words of R.C. Sproul:

> If we had any compassion for other people, we would wail at the thought of a single one of them falling into the pit of hell. We could not stand to hear the cries of the damned for five seconds. To be exposed to God's fury for a moment would be more than we could bear. To contemplate it for eternity is too awful to consider.[29]

Charles Spurgeon also has a call for Christians to warn those who are perishing:

> Oh, my brothers and sisters in Christ, if sinners will be damned, at least let them leap to hell over our bodies; and if they will perish, let them perish with our arms about their knees, imploring them to stay, and not madly to destroy themselves. If hell must be filled, at least let it be filled in the teeth of our exertions, and

> let not one go there unwarned and unprayed for.[30]

The magician Penn Jillette, who is sadly an atheist, has made remarks that I find thought-provoking. He gives his thoughts on whether or not Christians should share their faith:

> I've always said that I don't respect people who don't proselytize. I don't respect that at all. If you believe that there's a heaven and a hell, and people could be going to hell or not getting eternal life, and you think that it's not really worth telling them this because it would make it socially awkward—and atheists who think people shouldn't proselytize and who say just leave me along [sic] and keep your religion to yourself—how much do you have to hate somebody to not proselytize? How much do you have to hate somebody to believe everlasting life is possible and not tell them that?... I mean, if I believed, beyond the shadow of a doubt, that a truck was coming at you, and you didn't believe that truck was bearing down on you, there is a certain point where I tackle you. And this is more important than that.[31]

Telling people the Good News of Jesus Christ is indeed the most loving thing you can do. Some may deem it hateful, or intrusive, or weird, but the true hateful action would be not to share. There will be resistance and persecution, but we must fear God on behalf of those who don't.

If God sent himself as Jesus to take our eternal punishment

for us, then why can't we as his followers tell our neighbors and co-workers about him? The Joshua Project estimates that there are over 3 billion people who have never heard of Jesus, nor do they have access to Christian resources.[32] What can you do to change that? What would be tangible next steps in your life to make Jesus known to the world?

* * *

To summarize this chapter: An important part of fearing God's chastisement is fearing God's judgment. Christians and non-Christians alike should meditate on God's judgment. God will judge the works of saints and the sins of the wicked. The place of eternal judgment for the wicked is hell. Hell is an eternal place of torment, isolation, and hopelessness. God demonstrates his mercy and his justice by sending Jesus, the Lamb of God, to take away our sins and offer us eternal life with him. Rightly fearing God's judgment should produce repentance, obedience, love for God, and compassion for those under his judgment. We fear God by believing and sharing the Good News of Jesus.

6

The Authority of Jesus

We have covered a lot of ground in our discussion of biblical and beautiful fear of the Lord. In the first chapter we looked at who we are and how we relate to fear. We also introduced the biblical mandate to fear God. The last couple of chapters took a deep dive into different aspects of fear and how they relate to God's character.

Moving forward, I will spend a few chapters investigating how fear relates to the Trinity. Do we fear each member of the Godhead the same? Or, to put it another way, do the unique roles of the Father, Son, and Spirit affect how and why we relate to them in fear? My goal here is not to theorize at the mystery of the Trinity, or to unwrap all the responsibilities and qualities of each member. Rather, my goal is to gain insight into a proper fear for each person of our triune God.

In this chapter, the spotlight is on Jesus - the Son of God. There are three main purposes of this chapter. In order to have a healthy fear of Jesus, we must first understand the opposition to fearing Him. Next, I will showcase the aspects of Jesus that are meant to invoke fear and help us ponder how we might respond to these truths. Finally, we want to know how to follow Jesus' example in fearing God.

Opposition to Jesus is rampant. In fact, the concept of rightly fearing Jesus is foreign to the world. In movies and TV shows, the name of Jesus Christ is turned into a slur; a phrase meant to communicate surprise or disgust. Those who use Jesus' name as a slur profane the name of the Son of God. They dishonor the one to whom "every knee shall bow" (Romans 14:11), and the "name that is above every name" (Philippians 2:9) "by which we must be saved" (Acts 4:12). The fear of God in Jesus is absent from the lips of the culture around us.

Among followers of Jesus, the idea of fearing him may be lacking as well. We may overemphasize that Jesus had "no form or majesty that we should look at him, and no beauty that we should desire him. He was despised and rejected by men, a man of sorrows and acquainted with grief; and as one from whom men hide their faces he was despised, and we esteemed him not" (Isaiah 53:1b-3). A man of sorrows? That doesn't sound like someone we would fear. Furthermore, in Jesus' own words, he is "gentle and lowly in heart" (Matthew 11:29). Surely someone describing themselves in such a way shouldn't be feared. If that weren't enough, we also know that Jesus loved us enough to give his life for us. Why fear someone who sacrificially loves us?

It can be easy to think of Jesus as *only* kind, loving, meek, gentle, and lowly. These are all 100% true characteristics of the Son of God, but if we overemphasize these qualities, we may forget that Jesus is also the "King of kings and Lord of lords" (Revelation 19:16). He has limitless power and authority. Jesus dwells in heaven enthroned in unapproachable light and magnificent glory. When Jesus gloriously appeared to his friend

John on the island of Patmos, John "fell at his feet as though dead" (Revelation 1:17). If we saw Jesus in his glory, we would be terribly frightened.

In C.S. Lewis' fictional book *The Lion, the Witch, and the Wardrobe*, there is a lion named Aslan, who represents Jesus. At one point in the story, four siblings - Peter, Susan, Edmund, and Lucy - are told for the first time about Aslan by Mr. and Mrs. Beaver. Naturally, the siblings begin asking the beavers questions about Aslan:

> "Is—is he a man?" asked Lucy.
>
> "Aslan a man!" said Mr. Beaver sternly. "Certainly not. I tell you he is the King of the wood and the son of the great Emperor-beyond-the-Sea. Don't you know who is the King of Beasts? Aslan is a lion—*the* Lion, the great Lion."
>
> "Ooh!" said Susan, "I'd thought he was a man. Is he—quite safe? I shall feel rather nervous about meeting a lion."
>
> "That you will, dearie, and no mistake," said Mrs. Beaver; "if there's anyone who can appear before Aslan without their knees knocking, they're either braver than most or else just silly."
>
> "Then he isn't safe?" said Lucy.
>
> "Safe?" said Mr. Beaver; "don't you hear what Mrs. Beaver tells you? Who said anything about safe? 'Course he isn't safe. But he's good. He's the King, I tell you."[33]

Over the next few pages, I pray we come to the conclusion that Jesus isn't safe. That should cause us to fear him. Yet, we must also draw near to him because of his goodness. This thought is well summarized by A.W. Tozer; who wrote, "The greatness of God rouses fear within us, but His goodness encourages us not to be afraid of Him. To fear and not be afraid - that is the paradox of faith."[34]

What are the specific qualities about Jesus that should cause us to fear Him? They are all related to his authority: *We must fear Jesus because of his authority as the Righteous Judge, his authority as the Word of God, and his authority as the worker of miracles and forgiver of sins.*

Jesus the Righteous Judge

We have already established that God will judge everyone. There is a final judgment that will be revealed at the end of history when God will judge the works of the saints and the sins of the wicked.

How is God to carry out his judgment?

The book of Revelation is where we find our key text for this section. In this book, John is given visions from Jesus that he is told to write down. These revelations are largely about the end of the world and the establishment of the new heaven and new earth, where there will be no sin or evil.

There are many differing views on eschatology that are derived from the book of Revelation. Many are valuable and useful to examine, but I think the best thing that you can come away with from reading Revelation is the greatness of God in Jesus Christ. From chapter 6, we see his greatness on full display:

> When he opened the sixth seal, I looked, and behold, there was a great earthquake, and the sun became black as sackcloth, the full moon became like blood, and the stars of the sky fell to the earth as the fig tree sheds its winter fruit when shaken by a gale. The sky vanished like a scroll that is being rolled up, and every mountain and island was removed from its place. Then the kings of the earth and the great ones and the generals and the rich and the powerful, and everyone, slave and free, hid themselves in the caves and among the rocks of the mountains, calling to the mountains and rocks, "Fall on us and hide us from the face of him who is seated on the throne, and from the wrath of the Lamb, for the great day of their wrath has come, and who can stand?" (Revelation 6:12-17)

The Lamb - Jesus Christ - dramatically appears on the scene, and all the inhabitants of the world who do not belong to him are terribly afraid of his judgment and wrath. Notice their language. They are wishing for death in order to avoid facing God's wrath. Here we see that the final judgments of God are carried out by Jesus, and people are terrified.

This detail in Revelation 6 is not isolated. There are two other books in the Bible that bear witness to the fact that Jesus is the Righteous Judge. In the book of John, Jesus said this about himself: "For the Father judges no one, but has given all judgment to the Son... And he has given him authority to execute judgment, because he is the Son of Man" (John 5:22,27). From this we may glean that Jesus is the Judge because of his Father. God the Father gives the authority of judgment to God the Son. Therefore, Jesus' status as Judge is divinely appointed and eternally secured. There are no ifs, ands, or buts about it; he is the Judge.

The other book that speaks to Jesus as Judge is the book of Acts. In Acts we read, "And he [Jesus] commanded us to preach to the people and to testify that he is the one appointed by God to be judge of the living and the dead" (Acts 10:42). Again, we are told that God the Father has given Jesus the authority to judge. Another insight from Acts is that Jesus is the judge of the living *and* the dead. This is an all-inclusive judgment. Living and dead means everybody.

In Acts 17:31, Paul - speaking of God - continues this thought: "because he has fixed a day on which he will judge the world in righteousness by a man whom he has appointed; and of this he has given assurance to all by raising him from the dead." Paul is saying here that Jesus' resurrection from the dead is *proof* that Jesus is the Righteous Judge. Because he died and is alive again he is able to judge the living and the dead.

Jesus is uniquely qualified to judge humanity, since he is not only fully God, but also fully human. Jesus refers to himself as the "Son of Man". This is a reference to Daniel's prophecy in Daniel 7:13-14. According to this prophecy, God gives the Son of Man an everlasting dominion, heavenly glory, and an indestructible kingdom. By identifying himself as the Son of Man, Jesus reaffirms his humanity while also asserting his position as humanity's judge.

Being human is not enough to be the judge of all time. So what is different about Jesus? Jesus is the *perfect* human. There was no fault in him. He is sinless and spotless. If a random person were to judge me, and I were to respond in earthly pride, I might get defensive and think, "Who are they to judge me? Look at their life. They are no better." This doesn't fly with Jesus. He *is* better. When I look at the holy life of Jesus, I am forced to admit that he alone has every right to judge my actions and thoughts.

Finally, we should fear the authority of Jesus as Righteous Judge because he knows who we are. You may be able to fool me about how kind you are, or how generous or loving, but you cannot fool Jesus. He knows everything about you. The Gospels tell us that Jesus "knew what was in man" (John 2:25), and that he knew the thoughts of those around him (Matthew 9:4).

Think of the worst thing you've ever done. Jesus knows what it is. He was fully aware of your worst when he died for you. His love is not conditional on how messed up you are. This is a source of great comfort. However, if you reject his love and his sacrifice, he still knows all your faults; and his judgment remains. Jesus is the Righteous Judge, who lived the perfect sinless life and was raised from the grave to judge the living and the dead. He is appointed by the Father to have the authority as Judge, and his judgment brings wrath and despair. Jesus the Judge is rightly to be feared.

Jesus the Word of God

> He is clothed in a robe dipped in blood, and the name by which he is called is The Word of God.
> (Revelation 19:13)

This description of Jesus toward the end of Revelation identifies him as the Word of God. Note that it does not say that Jesus is *like* the Word of God, or that he *resembles* the Word of God, but that he *is* the Word of God.

This might cause your head to spin at first, but thankfully, the same author who wrote Revelation – John – also wrote the

Gospel of John. Here, he provides more clarity to this concept of Jesus as the Word of God: "In the beginning was the Word, and the Word was with God, and the Word was God. He was in the beginning with God. All things were made through him, and without him was not any thing made that was made... And the Word became flesh and dwelt among us, and we have seen his glory, glory as of the only Son from the Father, full of grace and truth" (John 1:1-3, 14).

In the context of John 1, Jesus and the Word are interchangeable. Imagine John's words like this: In the beginning was Jesus, and Jesus was with God, and Jesus was God. And Jesus became flesh and dwelt among us, and we have seen his glory, glory as of the only Son from the Father, full of grace and truth.

Jesus is not only God in the flesh, but he is also the Word of God in the flesh - a Word full of grace and truth. In Genesis 1, at the beginning, when God speaks the universe into existence, it is the Word of God. Within the narrative of creation, the repeated phrase "And God said" (Genesis 1:3, 6, 9, 11, 14, 20, 24, 28, 29) refers to the Word of God and the person of Jesus. God's powerful acts of creation were spoken through his Word, Jesus. This Word speaks life and beauty out of darkness and chaos.

Now for the obvious question: Why should we fear the Word of God? In short, we should fear the Word of God because fearing God's Word brings benefits to our lives. Among those benefits are good judgment and discernment. It is the Word of God which directs our hearts toward good and convicts our hearts of evil.

One of the many benefits of fearing God's Word is found in Isaiah 66:2 where God says, "But this is the one to whom I will look: he who is humble and contrite in spirit and trembles at my word." In other words, God shows regard for those who have regard for his Word. Not only does fearing God's Word bring the favor of God, but it has many other blessings as shown in Psalm 19:

> The law of the LORD is perfect, reviving the soul; the testimony of the LORD is sure, making wise the simple; the precepts of the LORD are right, rejoicing the heart; the commandment of the LORD is pure, enlightening the eyes; the fear of the LORD is clean, enduring forever; the rules of the LORD are true, and righteous altogether. (Psalm 19:7-9)

In this Psalm of David, the fear of the Lord is listed right along with many different categories of the Word of God: the law, testimony, precepts, commandment, and rules of the Lord. This comparison essentially communicates that the words of God and the fear of God are inseparable.

Now re-read the passage and see what is being articulated: The Word of God, along with the fear of the Lord, brings revival to the soul, wisdom, rejoicing, and enlightenment (i.e. understanding). These are all wonderful benefits.

Psalm 19 goes on to say that Scripture is used to warn us (verse 11). This is another benefit of revering the Word of God. It is expounded upon in Hebrews 4:12 which says, "For the word of God is living and active, sharper than any two-edged sword, piercing to the division of soul and of spirit, of joints and of marrow, and discerning the thoughts and intentions of the heart." God's Word is poignant in its warnings against sinful thoughts.

The idea of God's Word as a weapon is not isolated to Hebrews. Ephesians 6:17 also makes reference to the Word of God as the "sword of the Spirit". This sword is one of the tools by which we stand firm in our faith.

If you have watched movies such as *The Lord of the Rings* or *The Pirates of the Caribbean*, then you know the effect that a sharp sword can have. Swords are effective for stabbing, slashing, and decapitating. They are useful for defense and offense. The Word of God is sharper than any physical sword, because swords can only puncture flesh and bone. The Word of God punctures our souls, and it reveals to us our deepest desires and the condition of our hearts.

Although the Word of God is always essential and beneficial in our lives, the conviction that it brings may sometimes feel like a fatal stabbing. This is, of course, meant for our sanctification; but it should increase our fear and reverence for the Word. Whether we like it or not, this Word is the ultimate authority over our lives.

Not only does God's Word warn us of sin, it also gives us the knowledge to fight that sin and to stand firm in our faith. We have a powerful offensive and defensive weapon in the Word of God, if only we have enough reverence and fear to make use of it.

Now that we have taken a look at the benefits of fearing God's Word, let's step into a story from Scripture that demonstrates what fearing God's Word looks like. The narrative in 2 Kings 22 shows us the significant impact of fearing God's Word:

One of the last kings of the nation of Judah was King Josiah. During his reign, he ordered the high priest Hilkiah to repair the temple of God. As a result of this operation, Hilkiah found the Book of the Law - Deuteronomy - in the temple. Hilkiah gave it to the secretary Shaphan, who read it before King Josiah.

When Josiah heard these words, he tore his clothes and wept. He now knew that the nation of Judah had not obeyed the laws of God. He understood that they would face God's wrath for turning aside from God's rules and serving idols. Josiah immediately sent Hilkiah and others to inquire of God. They visited the prophetess Huldah who spoke on the Lord's behalf.

She told them that God would indeed punish Judah and bring disaster upon it. However, she also said that God heard the cries of King Josiah. Because the king was penitent and his heart turned to the Lord, God would not bring disaster upon the nation during the king's lifetime. God would allow Josiah to live out his life in peace. Josiah continued to walk in the ways of God and to do what was right throughout his reign as king.

If you can get past the difficult-to-pronounce names, consider the heart posture of the king. Within this narrative, King Josiah *found* and *feared* God's Word. He believed the words that were written. Josiah repented and humbled himself on behalf of the nation. He realized the severity of not obeying God's words. As a result, God heard his cries, and promised peace in Judah during Josiah's reign. May we fear the Word of God as Josiah did!

I close this section with words from John Bunyan. John Bunyan wrote extensively on the fear of the Lord. He understood the consequences of not fearing God's Word, as well as the satisfaction that comes from this fear. This is his charge to us:

> God's people should stand more in fear of the Word of God than all the terrors of the world. Even in the hearts of God's people today, there is not the proper respect and appreciation that there should be for the Word of God. This lack of reverence of the Word is the reason for all the chaos in the believer's heart,

life, walk, and fellowship with other Christians...[35] A man who drinks good doctrine into his soul fears God. If he drinks a lot, he fears a lot. If he drinks only a little, he fears God only a little. If he does not drink at all, he does not fear God at all. This teaches us how to recognize who fears the Lord. They are those who learn from and stand in awe of the Word of God. Those who have the holy Word of God engraved on the tablet of their heart fear God.[36]

Jesus the Miracle Worker

Many miracles were performed during Jesus' earthly ministry. Miracles defy the laws of nature, and are typically restorative. In order to perform a miracle, you need authority over nature. Jesus has that authority.

In this section, we are going to look at four distinct accounts of Jesus' miracles recorded in Scripture. These stories will acquaint us with the authority of Jesus and people who feared Jesus because of his authority. Miracles aside, I hope to highlight the different fear responses that people exhibit when confronted with miracles of Jesus. Perhaps we may learn a thing or two about how to fear Jesus in a healthy way.

The first miracle is the story of Jesus walking on water. This is recorded in Matthew 14:25-33, Mark 6:45-51, and John 6:16-21. The disciples of Jesus were crossing the Sea of Galilee in a boat, and the day was ending. Soon, the wind picked up and the sea turned harsh. After sailing for a few miles in hazardous conditions, the disciples noticed someone alongside the boat.

At first they thought they were seeing a ghost, and were terrified. It was not a ghost, however, but Jesus walking on the water.

One of the disciples - Peter - asked if Jesus would command him to come out on the water, and Jesus obliged. Peter walked out on the surface of the water with Jesus. This was short-lived, however, because Peter began to fear the wind and the waves. He began to waiver in his faith that Jesus could uphold him. This caused Peter to fall beneath the waves, so Jesus pulled him up, and the other disciples helped them both into the boat. Immediately, the wind stopped, the waves died down, and they arrived at their destination.

The highlighted miracle in this story is Jesus walking on the surface of the water as if it were solid ground. His disciples were understandably afraid when they saw him. The crux of the matter is in Peter's response. In his fear, Peter moved *toward* Jesus out onto the stormy sea. When Peter was afraid of that which was not Jesus (the wind and waves), he sank.

Healthy fear will bring us closer to Jesus. In our own lives, we should get out of our boats and move toward Jesus; even if stepping onto the sea seems impossible or we are in the midst of a storm. The alternative is that we allow our fear of Jesus to keep us in the boat, or we begin sinking because we chose to fear other things.

The second miracle to examine is the healing of a woman with a constant discharge of blood. This is recorded in Matthew 9:20-22, Mark 5:25-34, and Luke 8:43-48. Here, Jesus and his disciples were surrounded by a crowd that was pressing in on them. He was on his way to the house of a man whose daughter had just died.

In the midst of this crowd, there was a woman who had suffered from a blood discharge for twelve years. Despite spending all her money on doctors, her condition was growing worse. This woman must have had some idea of the power and authority of Jesus, because she decided to try getting close enough to Jesus to touch his clothes. She was convinced that upon touching the garments of Jesus, she would be made well. This woman had faith.

Sure enough, she was instantly healed of her disease the moment she touched Jesus. This caused her to fear and tremble. Divine power had gone out from Jesus and healed her. Jesus, wanting her to reveal herself, asked the crowd around him who had touched him. His disciples thought this was silly, as the crowd was so close that many people were touching him. Yet the woman, still afraid and trembling, came before Jesus and fell at his feet. Then, in the presence of the large crowd, she proclaimed how Jesus had healed her.

Here again we see that fear of Jesus is meant to draw us closer to Jesus. The woman's fear of Jesus was only outdone by her faith in Jesus. Her story begs these questions for us: When Jesus brings healing into our lives; do we faithlessly deny his work, or do we take a heart posture that humbly falls at his feet? Do we stay anonymous in the crowd, or do we tell the multitudes what Jesus has done for us? Fearing Jesus rightly is meant to be accompanied by faith. It is meant to bring us humbly before Jesus. This fear then empowers us to tell others how much Jesus has done for us.

The third miracle to examine is Jesus healing the blind and the lame in the temple. This is recorded in Matthew 21:12-17, Mark 11:15-19, and Luke 19:45-48. It is an interesting event, because the healing is preceded by Jesus doing something that caused quite a stir.

In this story, Jesus went to the Jewish temple in Jerusalem, and was distraught to see merchants and money changers set up at tables within the temple. With livestock and other goods for sale, it appeared to be a full blown marketplace. Jesus, being the Son of God, passionately declared that they had made his Father's house a den of robbers, when it was supposed to be a house of prayer for all nations.

Jesus began to drive the merchants and money changers out of the temple, along with their livestock. He flipped over their tables and chairs and he poured out their coins onto the ground. After effectively closing up shop for the day, a crowd began to form around Jesus there in the temple. He then began to heal the blind and the lame. He also began to teach about his authority. These miracles and teachings caused the crowd to be astonished at the wonderful things they were seeing and hearing. They were even singing praises to Jesus.

Here is where fear plays into this story: The chief priests and the scribes were present during this whole ordeal. Rather than believe in Jesus, they perceived him as a threat to their power. He had disrupted their influence and lifestyle. He was gaining a following. Therefore, the religious elite hated him. They did not have a godly fear. We know this because Scripture tells us that they were seeking to destroy Jesus. Out of their fear of Jesus, they sought to suppress Jesus' influence, entrap him, slander him, and kill him.

This begs a question for us: do we fear the authority of Jesus in a way that causes us to resent him? What we have seen in this story is an example of unhealthy, sinful fear. Michael Reeves wrote extensively on sinful fear in his book *Rejoice and Tremble: The Surprising Good News of the Fear of the Lord*:

> Sinful fear drives you *away* from God. This is the fear of the unbeliever who hates God, who remains a rebel at heart, who fears being exposed as a sinner and so runs from God. This is the fear of God that is at odds with love for God. It is the fear that is, instead, rooted in the very heart of sin. Dreading, opposing, and retreating from God, this fear generates the doubt that rationalizes unbelief. It is the motor for both atheism and idolatry, inspiring people to invent alternative 'realities' in place of the living God.[37]

In our last miracle, we will see both sinful fear and godly fear of Jesus. It is recorded in Matthew 8:28-34, Mark 5:1-20, and Luke 8:26-39. In this account, we witness the authority that Jesus has over demons.

Jesus and his disciples arrived on a boat to the countryside of the Gerasenes, where a man possessed by demons came out from nearby tombs to meet them. This man was naked, and bore cuts on his skin from carving himself with stones. He would often make loud noises, and he was so fierce that people avoided traveling near him. He possessed demonic strength, and the demons within him had driven him out into the wilderness.

When Jesus saw the man, he commanded the unclean spirits to come out of him. These demons, knowing that Jesus was the Son of God who had authority over them, begged Jesus not to torture them or send them into hell. They instead asked Jesus if he would allow them to enter a herd of two thousand pigs on a nearby hillside. Jesus granted them permission. When the demons had entered the pigs, they immediately drove the pigs down a steep bank into the sea.

The herdsmen of the pigs saw what happened, and they went into the city and told people there of what had occurred. On account of this, a crowd from the city and the surrounding countryside came to see what happened and to see Jesus. What they saw when they arrived was a wonderful sight: The previously demon-possessed man was sitting at Jesus' feet, wearing clothes, and in a perfectly sane state of mind.

The people in the crowd, however, were overcome with fear. They begged Jesus to get in his boat and leave the region. Jesus decided to depart. The man who had been healed of demon possession, however, desperately wanted to sail away with Jesus. Jesus instead instructed the man to tell his friends and family how Jesus had been merciful to him. This man proceeded to proclaim this good news not just to his friends and family, but also in the surrounding ten cities.

Did you catch the two responses to this miraculous display of Jesus' power? The man who was healed had a healthy fear. How do we know this? Because he desired to follow Christ and to obey him. He went and told of God's deliverance to his people. The crowd from the Gerasenes had unhealthy fear. They wanted Jesus to get as far away from them as possible. It's a bad day when you tell Jesus to go away and he obliges. Does your fear of Jesus' authority beckon you to follow him in obedience and sit at his feet? Or does your fear of Jesus' authority cause you to shrink back from his presence? Are you like the man who was freed from demons or the crowd from the Gerasenes?

Think back on the responses to the four miracles we have just examined: Peter's wavering fear, the woman's faithful fear, the religious leaders' hateful fear, and the mixed fear response on the countryside of the Gerasenes. In all these accounts, it is easy to categorize the reactions as either healthy fear or unhealthy fear.

Healthy fear draws us closer to Jesus. It guides us to walk with him in faith and let him into our lives. This fear causes us to come near to him, and to proclaim his goodness to the people around us. When we sit, we sit at the feet of Jesus. When we walk, we walk in obedience to his words. Healthy fear increases our intimacy with Christ.

Unhealthy fear separates us from Jesus. It brings terror and distress into our hearts. It says to Jesus, "Stay away from me!" and rejects his authority on our lives. With unhealthy fear, we ultimately find ourselves seeking to suppress the influence of Jesus, and wishing to destroy him. This fear cuts off the relationship that Christ wants to have with us.

Depending on where our fear of God drives us, the outcome can be either delightful or deadly. I close this discussion with a fitting quote from Charles Spurgeon's sermon "Five Fears":

> Nothing can be worse than this sinful fear; it hath slaughtered its myriads and sent thousands to hell. But yet it may seem a paradox; fear, when rightly employed, is the very brightest state of Christianity, and is used to express all piety, comprehended in one emotion. "The fear of God" is the constant description which the Scripture gives of true religion.[38]

Jesus the Forgiver of Sins

> But with you there is forgiveness,
>   that you may be feared. (Psalm 130:4)

Another key element to Jesus' earthly ministry, besides miracles, was the forgiveness of sins. Today, Jesus is still in the forgiveness business. Any sin is a grievous offense against God, yet God offers us the gift of being forgiven. Jesus, as God in the flesh, has the authority to forgive our sins.

Psalm 130:4 is a verse that has caused me much contemplation. I was intrigued with the notion that God's forgiveness could prompt fear. One might think that the forgiveness of God breeds the opposite of fear: calmness, assurance, and bliss. This remained a mystery to me until God directed my attention to the story of Jesus healing the paralytic.

Within this story is yet another miracle, and it can be found in Matthew 9:1-7, Mark 2:1-12, and Luke 5:17-26. Matthew's account of what Jesus did is as follows:

> And getting into a boat he crossed over and came to his own city. And behold, some people brought to him a paralytic, lying on a bed. And when Jesus saw their faith, he said to the paralytic, "Take heart, my son; your sins are forgiven." And behold, some of the scribes said to themselves, "This man is blaspheming." But Jesus, knowing their thoughts, said, "Why do you think evil in your hearts? For which is easier, to say, 'Your sins are forgiven,' or to say, 'Rise and walk'? But that you may know that the Son of Man has authority on earth to forgive sins"—he then said to

the paralytic—"Rise, pick up your bed and go home."
And he rose and went home. When the crowds saw
it, they were afraid, and they glorified God, who had
given such authority to men.

(Matthew 9:1-7)

Jesus presented the scribes with a deductive argument that showcases the truth: If Jesus has authority to heal a paralytic of their paralysis, then he also has authority to forgive sins. Herein lies the answer to why forgiveness should cause us to fear God. The answer is in the authority of Jesus.

The crowd became fearful when they saw that the man who had been paralyzed was now restored to full functionality. Their fear caused them to glorify God. But before the man was physically healed, Jesus forgave him of his sins. Forgiveness was the man's greatest need. This was a much greater feat and somehow that in itself did not cause the crowd to have fear. Why? Because they only saw the physical miracle, and not the spiritual miracle.

When God says, "I forgive you," it is nothing short of a miracle. What this story shows us is that when Jesus performs a visible miracle, it is accompanied by an invisible miracle. If we could see the transformation in our souls upon being healed by divine forgiveness, we would be completely awestruck. Thus, a healthy fear of Jesus reminds us that his forgiveness is the greatest miracle we will ever witness. This fear invites us to draw near and worship him.

Jesus our Example

Because Jesus is the perfect human, he is not only the rightful object of our fear, but he is also our example of how to delight in fearing God. A prophecy about Jesus recorded in Isaiah 11:3 states, "And his delight shall be in the fear of the LORD." If we want to have a fear of God that is both biblical and beautiful, we must align ourselves with the example we are given in the life and death of Christ.

Knowing how to delight in fearing God really isn't that difficult when you look at the life of Jesus. Next time you read through the Gospels - Matthew, Mark, Luke, and John - ask yourself questions such as these:

- How did Jesus pray?
- How did Jesus love people?
- How did Jesus deal with temptation?
- How did Jesus handle sorrow and rejection?
- Whose approval did Jesus seek?
- What did Jesus teach his disciples?

Finding answers to these questions and then applying them to your life is a sure path to following Jesus more closely and fearing God rightly. As Christ delights in the fear of the Lord, may we also delight in the fear of the Lord.

The shocking part about this is that we know the outcome of a God-fearing life: It brings about death. Christ's life was laid down when he was gruesomely executed on a cross. He *chose* to lay his life down. This is our fearless example of how to live a God-fearing life. Listen to Jesus' words:

And calling the crowd to him with his disciples, he said to them, "If anyone would come after me, let him deny himself and take up his cross and follow me. For whoever would save his life will lose it, but whoever loses his life for my sake and the gospel's will save it." (Mark 8:34-35)

Jesus expects that his followers will continually die to themselves. This can be scary, but he promises us that there is life to be found in self-denial. We know this to be true because Jesus took up his own cross, died on it, and was raised from the dead. He offers us eternal life with him if we choose to follow him and to die to ourselves. Dietrich Bonhoeffer beautifully articulates this truth:

> The cross is laid on every Christian. The first Christ-suffering which every man must experience is the call to abandon the attachments of this world. It is that dying of the old man which is the result of his encounter with Christ. As we embark upon discipleship we surrender ourselves to Christ in union with his death—we give over our lives to death. Thus it begins; the cross is not the terrible end to an otherwise god-fearing and happy life, but it meets us at the beginning of our communion with Christ. When Christ calls a man, he bids him come and die.[39]

* * *

Ultimately, the fear of Jesus comes down to his authority over all things. Jesus has authority as the Righteous Judge who will return one day. Jesus has authority as the Word of God, who instructs our lives and discerns our hearts. Jesus has authority as the Miracle Worker, who by his power beckons us to draw near to him in faith and obedience. Jesus alone has the authority to forgive our sins before God. All of this should cause us to glorify him with every ounce of our being.

Jesus is our example in how to delight in godly fear. In order to delight in the fear of the Lord, we are to align ourselves with the life and death of Jesus.

This fear of the Lord is impossible in our own strength. On our own, we cannot adequately fear God in the way Jesus shows us. We need a Divine Helper...

7

Empowerment of the Spirit

In the summer of 2022, a few friends and I spontaneously planned a ten day vacation in Europe. We spent time in both the United Kingdom and in Switzerland. It was the trip of a lifetime.

I had hoped to visit these areas for quite a while, and I was fortunate enough to chase this adventure with some of my best friends. Together, we did all the typical tourist things: Stroll through the streets of London, enjoy a boat tour of Lake Geneva, explore the Scottish Highlands and old castles, consume bits of history in museums and churches, and meet fascinating new people.

For the duration of the trip, there was one item that I guarded more closely than anything else. No, it wasn't my phone, my wallet, or my toothbrush. The most valuable and influential item that I carried on that trip was the one that confirmed my identity: My passport.

As an American citizen, while I was going through customs in both countries, all I needed to do was simply present my passport, and I was granted entrance. If I ran into any issues during my stay, I could show up at the American embassy with my passport and they would offer me assistance. I always kept my passport close.

Passports are crucial for being in a foreign land. You *need* your passport. It gives you an authoritative identity as a citizen of your country, and it opens up doors to you that were previously closed. It gives you confidence to travel knowing that your country has your back. Having a passport allows you to live a life that you otherwise could not.

When I compare these benefits to those given by God, the similarities are striking. What member of the Trinity gives us confidence in our identity as a citizen of God's Kingdom? Who is it that goes with you wherever you are and enables you to experience a new life that pleases God? The Holy Spirit.

The Holy Spirit is the person of the Trinity that will be the focus of this chapter. There are many terms in the Bible that communicate who he is: Holy Spirit, Holy Ghost, Helper, Spirit of Truth, and Spirit of God. He dwells within every believer in Christ.

We cannot fear God in the way he intends without the help of his Spirit within us. The Holy Spirit has a vital role in empowering us to have a healthy fear of God. Before we investigate how the Holy Spirit fulfills this specific role, it is essential to understand what his role is on a larger scale. We can then take a closer look into three ways the Holy Spirit enables us to have a healthy fear of God:

1. The Holy Spirit imparts wisdom and truth to us from the mind of Christ.
2. The Holy Spirit empowers us with resurrection life.
3. The Holy Spirit gives us divine fear that draws us closer to God the Father.

After feasting on these truths, we will briefly discuss how to be filled with the Spirit and allow him to guide us in a healthy fear.

* * *

Since the Holy Spirit is the main focus of this section, let's take a second to shine a spotlight on the Holy Spirit's role *in general*. Other than direct truth from the Bible, one of the best resources for learning about the Holy Spirit is the book *The Holy Spirit: Activating God's Power in Your Life* by Billy Graham. In his book, Billy Graham has an excellent quote which clearly and succinctly describes the role of the Holy Spirit. He writes,

> The Holy Spirit is the one who reproves, convicts, strives, instructs, invites, quickens, regenerates, renews, strengthens, and uses. He must not be grieved, resisted, tempted, quenched, insulted, or blasphemed. He gives liberty to the Christian, direction to the worker, discernment to the teacher, power to the Word, and fruit to faithful service. He reveals the things of Christ. He teaches us how to use the sword of the Spirit, which is the Word of God. He guides us into all truth. He directs in the way of godliness. He teaches us how to answer the enemies of our Lord. He gives us access to the Father. He helps us in our prayer life.[40]

I hope your growing impression is that the Holy Spirit is *vital*. For understanding the Holy Spirit's role in general, there are four truths about the role of the Holy Spirit that will be helpful for the rest of this discussion.

First, the Holy Spirit's presence seals those who believe in Jesus. For the Christian, being sealed by the Holy Spirit means that our position as God's children is secured by the authority of God. Ephesians 1:13-14 says, "In him you also, when you heard the word of truth, the gospel of your salvation, and believed in him, were sealed with the promised Holy Spirit, who is the guarantee of our inheritance until we acquire possession of it, to the praise of his glory."

To get a picture of this seal, think of a wax stamp. I remember one of my sisters receiving a sealing wax kit with her first initial as a birthday present. Watching her seal a letter shut and stamp it with her mark is a vivid illustration of what it means to be secure in Christ. If you are a Christian, the Holy Spirit has stamped you with the authoritative mark of God. At the moment of belief in Christ, the Spirit of God invaded your soul and irreversibly declared that you belong to God.

Second, the Holy Spirit is the divine Helper who bears witness about Jesus. Jesus said in John 15:26, "But when the Helper comes, whom I will send to you from the Father, the Spirit of truth, who proceeds from the Father, he will bear witness about me." The Spirit tells our hearts the true identity of Jesus. He declares to us that Jesus is the Christ - God's Anointed One. In 1 John 4:2 we read, "By this you know the Spirit of God: every spirit that confesses that Jesus Christ has come in the flesh is from God." The witness of the Spirit of God, along with the testimony of the Word of God, is the only way we can know who Jesus really is.

Third, the Holy Spirit guides followers of Christ to know truth. John 16:13 states that "When the Spirit of truth comes, he will guide you into all the truth, for he will not speak on his own authority, but whatever he hears he will speak, and he will declare to you the things that are to come." There is no deception in the Spirit of God.

It is worth noting here that the Holy Spirit cares deeply for the truth. In Acts 5, God slays a man and his wife for lying to the Holy Spirit and testing God. This event should remind us to revere the Holy Spirit in a way that leads us to be truthful and to reject any form of deception.

Fourth and finally, the Holy Spirit brings conviction of sin. No soul has ever truly repented of their sin without first being convicted by the Spirit of God. That is what we see in the Bible: "And when he [The Holy Spirit] comes, he will convict the world concerning sin and righteousness and judgment" (John 16:8). The Holy Spirit convicts us by burdening us with the reality of our sin, the righteousness of God, the judgment we have earned, and the hope of forgiveness and eternal life.

I believe these truths are foundational to the Holy Spirit's work in our lives. Equipped with this knowledge of the Holy Spirit, we are now ready to review the Holy Spirit's role in our fear of God.

The Mind of Christ

One essential way the Holy Spirit leads us into healthy fear of the Lord is by imparting wisdom and truth to us from the mind of Christ. Jesus is our example in how to delight in the fear of the Lord. In order to follow Christ's example, we must adopt his mindset. This is the work of the Holy Spirit.

This idea of knowing the mind of Christ might sound rather far-fetched at first. It reminds me of my response to the icebreaker question, "If you could have a superpower, what would it be?" My typical answer is that I would want to read minds like Professor X from X-Men. Maybe that's not your cup of tea, and that's fine! My wife has informed me that it would be miserable to know what everyone is thinking. She may be right. To each, their own preferred superpower I suppose!

While this superpower is fun to imagine, I will never be able to know the mind of another person. And yet, what is impossible with man is possible with God. Through the Holy Spirit working in me, I am able to know the mind of Jesus Christ:

> For who knows a person's thoughts except the spirit of that person, which is in him? So also no one comprehends the thoughts of God except the Spirit of God. Now we have received not the spirit of the world, but the Spirit who is from God, that we might understand the things freely given us by God. And we impart this in words not taught by human wisdom but taught by the Spirit, interpreting spiritual truths to those who are spiritual.
>
> The natural person does not accept the things of the Spirit of God, for they are folly to him, and he is not able to understand them because they are spiritually discerned. The spiritual person judges all things, but is himself to be judged by no one. "For who has understood the mind of the Lord so as to instruct him?" But we have the mind of Christ.
>
> (1 Corinthians 2:11-16)

This passage from Paul's letter to the Corinthians lays out an incredible reality. Not only are we given God's Spirit, but we are also granted access by the Spirit to see a treasure trove of spiritual realities. This comes directly from the mind of God in Christ Jesus. Moreover, those who are more mature in the faith play a part in sharing truth that has been revealed to them with younger believers. They are able to spiritually discern things of the Spirit, and impart them to others.

Although this knowledge and wisdom brings joy and awe to followers of Jesus, the passage says that those who do not have the Spirit of God see these truths as foolishness. Unbelievers will say that spiritual truth from God makes no sense. They may call it hateful, or impossible, or downright evil. It may be labeled as lies or stupidity. This assessment is not a reflection on the credibility and wisdom of God, but rather a reflection of the dull hearts that choose not to believe.

Having the mind of Christ does not mean that Christians know *everything* that God knows. For many good reasons, that is not God's intent. Based on the text, the purpose of God in giving us the mind of Christ through his Spirit is fourfold:

1. We can understand what God has freely given us.
2. We can share wisdom and truth from the Spirit to others.
3. We may accept, discern, and understand the things of the Holy Spirit.
4. We may rightly judge all things.

Having the mind of Christ gives us the ability to think, speak and act more like him.

We have now come full circle: Jesus delights in the fear of the Lord, and while on earth he exhibited a healthy reverence for his Father. The mind of Christ, given by the Holy Spirit, enables us to do the same in our lives. This is the first way that the Holy

Spirit leads us into healthy fear of the Lord.

The early church recognized this link between fearing God and having a spiritual mind. Barnabas, one of the early church leaders, wrote, "Let us be spiritually-minded: let us be a perfect temple to God. As much as in us lies, let us meditate upon the fear of God, and let us keep His commandments, that we may rejoice in His ordinances."[41]

In his admonition for early Christians to be *spiritually-minded*, Barnabas tells them to carefully consider the *fear of the Lord*. May we present-day Christians consider his words as well.

Resurrection Life

The second way in which the Holy Spirit leads us into healthy fear of the Lord is through the power of resurrection life. Every year around Easter time, I like to set aside time to pray and meditate on Bible verses that speak of the resurrection of Jesus. One such verse is Romans 8:11: "If the Spirit of him who raised Jesus from the dead dwells in you, he who raised Christ Jesus from the dead will also give life to your mortal bodies through his Spirit who dwells in you."

Do you understand what this means for your life? The very same Spirit that once resurrected Christ from the dead is the Spirit that is with you *right now*. This is not a power you can control. The Holy Spirit isn't like the force in Star Wars, or like Peter Parker's spider-sense. Instead, he enables you to live to the glory of God.

The power of the Holy Spirit is within you in order that you might live a life that aligns with God's will. Our old life which brought about death, is now put to death. What remains in us is the life of Jesus; a life empowered by the Spirit.

This new life only comes through a radical transformation. Just as a caterpillar develops a chrysalis and emerges as a butterfly, we too will never again be the same. According to 2 Corinthians 5:17, "Therefore, if anyone is in Christ, he is a new creation. The old has passed away; behold, the new has come."

This spiritual transformation is a work of the Holy Spirit. He changes us by bringing us face-to-face with the truth, hope, and glory of the Lord Jesus: "And we all, with unveiled face, beholding the glory of the Lord, are being transformed into the same image from one degree of glory to another. For this comes from the Lord who is the Spirit" (2 Corinthians 3:18). As new creations, we are continually being transformed as we see the glory of Christ and rely on the Spirit.

Imagine showing up at the White House in Washington D. C. wearing stinky, worn out, and hole-ridden clothes. The fabric on your skin is itchy, dirty and ragged. You feel out of place and self-conscious standing on the marble floors with grand pillars that clearly show your shabby reflection. Now imagine that someone takes you aside and shows you the president's or first lady's own wardrobe. They clothe you with a fine suit or dress and send you on your way.

All of a sudden, you feel as if you belong. Your new clothes give you the confidence to go anywhere and talk to anyone. This is the type of transformation the Spirit does in us. Jesus likens having the Holy Spirit to wearing the strength of God. He told his disciples, "And behold, I am sending the promise of my Father upon you. But stay in the city until you are clothed with power from on high" (Luke 24:49). Receiving the Holy Spirit transforms us and clothes us with power to live the life that God has for us - a life that seeks the glory of God and rightly fears him.

Divine Fear

Being like-minded with Christ and being empowered with resurrection life should certainly inspire awe of God and a desire to honor him. However, the Holy Spirit's role in the fear of the Lord does not stop there.

The Holy Spirit himself gives us divine fear that draws us closer to God. In Isaiah 11:2, the Holy Spirit is described as the Spirit of wisdom, understanding, counsel, might, knowledge, and - get this - the fear of the Lord. These qualities of the Spirit work their way into those who are filled with the Spirit.

Since he is the Spirit of the fear of the Lord, everything he does will lead us with the fear of the Lord. When the Holy Spirit convicts us, he convicts us with the fear of the Lord. When the Holy Spirit helps us, he helps us into the fear of the Lord. If we are being transformed by the Spirit, then our fear of God and love for God will be ever-increasing.

It is at this point that some readers who know their Bibles may be confused, because a well-known verse about the Spirit is 2 Timothy 1:7, which says, "for God gave us a spirit not of fear but of power and love and self-control." If the Holy Spirit is the Spirit of the fear of the Lord in Isaiah 11, then why does Paul write in 2 Timothy that we are given a spirit not of fear but of power, love, and self-control?

Here is your answer: 2 Timothy 1 is talking about a fear of shame, imprisonment, and suffering for the sake of Christ. Read the whole chapter and it will be clear. The Spirit of God gives us the power, love, and self-control to proclaim the gospel with joy in the midst of persecution. The Holy Spirit causes us to fear God, and to overcome our fear of man.

In addition to filling us with fear of the Lord, the Holy Spirit also has a special role in our relationship to God the Father. Scripture tells us that having the Spirit of God makes us spiritual children of God and heirs in his kingdom:

> For all who are led by the Spirit of God are sons of God. For you did not receive the spirit of slavery to fall back into fear, but you have received the Spirit of adoption as sons, by whom we cry, "Abba! Father!" The Spirit himself bears witness with our spirit that we are children of God, and if children, then heirs—heirs of God and fellow heirs with Christ, provided we suffer with him in order that we may also be glorified with him. (Romans 8:14-17)

I don't want to encroach on our future discussion of God the Father, but suffice it to say that fearing God means having reverence for him as your good and loving Father. The Holy Spirit gives us an intimate connection with God as his adopted children. Commenting on this passage in Romans 8, John Bunyan wrote, "The godly fear from the Holy Spirit brings the Spirit of adoption. The soul is removed from the state and condition from which it has brought itself, by nature and sin, and is put into Christ. The soul is blessed with eternal life and grace."[42]

The Holy Spirit gives us the fear of God, and simultaneously removes our fear of man. To those who have received him through faith in Jesus, he is the Spirit of adoption. The Spirit of adoption affirms that we are children of God, and because of this we may now have earnest reverence and fear of God as his children. This reverence is a healthy fear; drawing us closer to our loving Father. It all proceeds from the Holy Spirit at work within us.

I hope you are filled with awe as you consider the vital role that the Holy Spirit plays in our lives. We are given knowledge of mysteries too great for the world to fathom, clothed with a power the world can only dream of and ushered into the loving arms of the One who loves us with fatherly abandon. These are incredible blessings far too wonderful to comprehend, and they are all by the power of the Holy Spirit. This should evoke the question, "How can I be more filled with the Spirit?"

Filled with the Spirit

Every believer is indwelt with the Holy Spirit, but not every believer is filled with the Spirit. To be filled with the Spirit is to be influenced by the will of God in every aspect of life – including the fear of the Lord. Based on Billy Graham's study of the New Testament, he wrote that there are three practical steps to being filled with the Holy Spirit:[43]

1. Develop an understanding and knowledge of the truth from God's Word.
2. Submit to God and accept his authority over your life.
3. Walk in faith and live out your belief in Jesus.

I think this is a great place to start in order to become filled with the Spirit and gain the subsequent blessings of fearing God. In order to take these steps in your life, there are three traits that you must embrace: *discipline*, *humility*, and *hope*.

Discipline is crucial to discerning truth from God's Word. This lifelong pursuit cannot be achieved without putting in the reps. Studying truth from the Bible takes *discipline*. Often, studying the Bible means early mornings, or late nights, or saying "NO!" to other things that compete for our time. It means taking notes and filling journals. It means reading commentaries and listening to sermons.

Most importantly, it means being disciplined in prayer. Praying God's Word is the ultimate method to discerning God's Word. This is not rocket science, but it does take time. Just as the athlete trains for competition by going to the gym often, we must train ourselves to be in the Word often in order to be filled with the Spirit.

Humility is non-negotiable if you are to submit to God and accept his authority over you. In case you were not aware, submission is not popular in society. Many young people today resist authority figures. It is unfortunate that this is the case, because submission has extreme value in our lives as it relates to God. To declare to God, "I submit to you." is an act of humility.

You cannot truly submit to God while strutting around in pride. Humility must be based on the truth found in step 1. Humility toward God recognizes the truth of who God is and the truth of who we are. It allows God to increase in our lives while we ourselves decrease. This fuels a blissful submission to God and to his way, and we are all better off for it. Who would you rather have running your life? Yourself (not all-powerful, not immortal, not all-knowing) or God (all-powerful, immortal, all-knowing)? Those who humble themselves before God put themselves in a position to be filled by the Spirit.

Hope means that you walk in faith and live out your belief in Jesus. Of course, I am not referring to physically walking. Walking in faith is spiritual. It means trusting what we can't see and believing what we don't understand. It requires action. We must make decisions based on the true promises that God has given to us.

For our hope to be genuine, it must be in what we can't see (Romans 8:24-25). Our hope must be in Jesus' life, death, resurrection, ascension, and return. The Spirit of God affirms this hope and fills us with it all the more.

How can you know if you are walking in the Spirit and allowing him to fill you? The Bible goes so far as to give us a method to gauge if we are filled with the Spirit:

> And do not get drunk with wine, for that is debauchery, but be filled with the Spirit, addressing one another in psalms and hymns and spiritual songs, singing and making melody to the Lord with your heart, giving thanks always and for everything to God the Father in the name of our Lord Jesus Christ, submitting to one another out of reverence for Christ. (Ephesians 5:18-21)

If you were to drink too much alcohol, it would begin to have control over you. In a much more positive sense, if you are filled with the Holy Spirit, he will begin to control your thoughts and actions. For the Christian, being filled with the Spirit is a sure way of being more like Jesus and delighting in the fear of God.

If you find yourself praising God, it is a good indicator that you are filled with the Spirit. If your praise of God is overflowing into your conversations with others, then chances are that you are filled with the Spirit. If you find that gratitude toward God is a common theme in your thought life, then most likely you are filled with the Spirit. If you bring humility and submission into your interactions with those in the church, then I'll bet you are filled with the Spirit. Related to the theme of this book, if you find yourself having a deep reverence for Christ, then this probably means that you are filled with the Spirit *and* you have a healthy fear of God.

So ask yourself: "Am I filled with the Spirit? Do I have a healthy fear of the Lord?" If the answer is no, I hope you will consider the tools and truths laid out in this chapter.

* * *

Take note of the profound blessings which have surfaced: The Holy Spirit dwells inside of those who follow Jesus. The Holy Spirit seals us as members of God's family. He is our Helper who bears witness about Jesus to us. He guides us into all truth and convicts us of our sins.

The Holy Spirit has a vital role in leading us into healthy fear of the Lord. He gives us the mind of Christ, empowers us with resurrection life, and grants us divine fear that draws us closer to God the Father as his children. By the discipline of knowing God's Word, humbly submitting to God, and having faith and hope in God, we can be filled with the Holy Spirit and begin to live in the fear of the Lord. May our fear be ever-increasing as we live by the Spirit.

8

Our Father's Discipline

When it comes to people I look up to, an obvious choice is my dad.

Throughout my life, my dad laid a strong foundation and built me up in ways that have greatly blessed me. Growing up, my dad went through Bible study books with me, and led our family in Scripture readings. He empowered me to embrace the unknown and step out in faith. As I grew to adulthood, my dad's mentorship became a constant friendship. He is a gentle man, but also firm; and these are qualities that I really admire.

I have two stories about my dad that demonstrate these qualities. When I was a freshman in college, one of my first priorities was to make friends. I eventually did find those friends, but this story picks up at one of my early attempts in the process. I had just invited around twenty people to join me at the theater for the new *Jason Bourne* movie. As it turned out, no one was able to join me.

There I sat in the theater; watching the pre-movie commercials all by myself. I got a text from my thoughtful dad asking me how it was going, so I informed him of my sad, lonely predicament. A few minutes later the room darkened and the commercials ended. Just as the movie started, my dad sat down next to me with a big bowl of popcorn! Like the liquefied butter on his popcorn, my heart was melted. My dad had dropped everything to come spend time with me when I was hurting. This is the gentleness that he has always shown to me and to others.

Gentleness is not the only quality my dad possesses. He is firm as well; not only in his beliefs, but also in his discipline. As a teenager, I experienced that discipline firsthand. I can't remember how many times Dad took my phone or keys away to teach me not to make stupid decisions. And believe me, I made stupid decisions in my teen years!

Being grounded stinks, but it taught me something: Because my dad loves me, he firmly disciplined me in an attempt to keep me safe, and healthy, and to guide me toward the ways of Jesus. If my dad wasn't firm with me, I would not have learned such valuable lessons that prepared me for the future.

Gentle and firm: These excellent qualities are not unlike those of our heavenly Father.

God the Father is the final person of the triune Godhead to be discussed regarding fear of the Lord. Our heavenly Father is loving, firm, and good. He lavishes blessings and good gifts upon those whom he loves. Because of his love, the Father also disciplines his children. We become children of God the Father by faith in Jesus.

When you think of the Father's discipline, it is important to draw a distinction from God's wrath. While both fall under the category of God's chastisement, they are different in object and purpose. The purpose of God's wrath is judgment of sin, and its objects are those in rebellion against God. Meanwhile the goal of his discipline is increased righteousness and holiness for his children - the objects of his love. The Father desires all his children to look and live like Jesus, and his perfect discipline guides us along this path. Here is the bottom line: If you are a child of God, you are no longer under the wrath of God, but you should still fear the discipline of God.

Because discipline is often accompanied with intense pain, the Father's discipline can be a fearful thing in our lives. Here is the question you must ask yourself as it relates to the Father's discipline: Do you fear the pain of God's discipline more than you revere your heavenly Father? If so, then you have an unhealthy fear of God's chastisement. On the contrary, having a healthy fear of God's chastisement means having deep reverence for your heavenly Father that transcends the fear of painful discipline and produces obedience.

A healthy reverence for God does not prevent fear of pain that comes with discipline. This too is healthy as long as your fear of pain is not greater than your reverence for God. Fear of pain protects us from doing all sorts of terrible things, but if that fear is not accompanied by a reverence for our Father, we will attempt to hide our deeds, and separate ourselves from God. When your fear of pain exceeds your fear of God, this becomes an unhealthy fear.

As we saw in chapter 3, an unhealthy fear of discipline is demonstrated in Genesis. After Adam and Eve disobeyed God's only command to them, Adam admits to God, "I heard the sound of you in the garden, and I was afraid, because I was naked, and I hid myself" (Genesis 3:10). As fallen humans, our natural response to God's discipline is to hide or distance ourselves from him.

In contrast, a proper fear of God's discipline leans into our identity as his children. Proverbs summarizes the truths about God that I hope we come to cherish deeply:

> My son, do not despise the LORD's discipline or be weary of his reproof, for the LORD reproves him whom he loves, as a father the son in whom he delights.
> (Proverbs 3:11-12)

If God is disciplining you, it is because he delights in you. Although his discipline seems wearisome and difficult, it is done in love.

As we dig deeper into the topic of the Father's discipline, we will uncover three layers of truth: We must understand *what* it means to be beloved children of God, we must understand *why* God disciplines his children, and we must understand *how* God disciplines his children. In my life, this has probably been the most transformational topic of this study on the fear of the Lord. So grab some coffee, get comfortable, and join me in discovering the richness of our Father's discipline.

Beloved Children of a Good Father

During my college years, I spent two summers overseas doing ministry in a foreign country. In that part of the world, there was and is significant hostility toward Christ. Persecution is common. As a result, certain security precautions were in order. One of those safety measures included minimizing the use of Christian vocabulary such as "Bible" or "church". To this end, my companions and I used the word "Father" instead of "God" so we wouldn't draw as much attention to ourselves.

The practice had unintended results. Even to this day, calling God "Father" has moved me. You can try it yourself! Just spend a day or a week replacing the word "God" with "Father" in most of your conversations. Here is what that did for me:

Referring to the creator of the universe as Father opened my mind to who I am serving and who I belong to. Each time I referred to God as "Father", my brain internalized the message "I am a child of God." It was a huge identity shift for me. In order for Christians to understand God's discipline and the fear of him, we must rely on the deepest identity we have - children of God.

This identity is confirmed by the other members of the Trinity. Recall our discussion of the Holy Spirit when we briefly touched on Romans 8:14-17. Verse 16 tells us that the Holy Spirit "himself bears witness with our spirit that we are children of God." God the Spirit tells us that we are children of God.

This is confirmed by God the Son as well. When Christ taught his disciples to pray, he told them to address God as *our* Father (Matthew 6:9). In this simple, yet profound instruction, Jesus identified those who follow him as children of God. The Spirit and the Son both bear witness that those who follow Christ are children of God the Father.

The Bible makes this truth abundantly clear, yet so often, we fail to remember. When I was a child, one of my favorite movies was the Disney film *The Lion King*. The story follows a young lion prince, Simba, who was wrongly accused for the death of his father, Mufasa. Simba was so full of shame that he ran away and thought he could never go back to his family.

At a critical moment when Simba was wrestling with his identity, Mufasa appeared to him in the stars. Instead of addressing the past, Simba's father gave him one command,

"Remember who you are. You are my son."[44] Refueled by his father's words, Simba returned home to make things right and step into his true identity. God gives us the same reminder:

> "and I will be a father to you, and you shall be sons and daughters to me, says the Lord Almighty." Since we have these promises, beloved, let us cleanse ourselves from every defilement of body and spirit, bringing holiness to completion in the fear of God.
> (2 Corinthians 6:18-7:1)

As we remember our identity as children of God, we are empowered to live out of this reality. This means we seek to be holy because God has promised us that we are children of a Holy God. Holiness is accomplished through the fear of the Lord working in our hearts as his children. Since we have the promise of God as our Father, we should live in obedience and submission out of reverence for him.

Not only are we children of God; we are *beloved* children of God. Consider the love that God the Father has for God the Son. Matthew records two instances where a voice from the sky spoke about Jesus. The voice was God the Father, and in both cases he proclaimed, "This is my beloved Son" (Matthew 3:17, 17:5). This message was broadcast from heaven so the world would know the deep joy and pleasure that Jesus brings his Father. It communicates that the Father loves his Son.

But his love doesn't stop there.

The Epistles say that we are "heirs of God and fellow heirs with Christ" (Romans 8:17) and that God has "predestined us for adoption to himself" (Ephesians 1:5). We are called to be "imitators of God as beloved children" (Ephesians 5:1). This means that through faith in Jesus, the Father's affection is shown not solely toward his only begotten Son, but also to you as his adopted child. The Father loves *you*.

Whatever your biological father is like, know this: you have a good Father in heaven. He is the best Father, and he loves all his children who are his through faith in Christ. I am utterly amazed that God invites us into his family and into his loving embrace.

Discipline: The Why

With our identity as beloved children of God firmly established, we now come face-to-face with this question: If God loves us as his children, why does he discipline us? While this question makes sense to our human minds, it really misses the whole point of discipline. What I hope we see here is this: God loves us, *therefore* he disciplines us.

Discipline, in general, always has a goal in mind. If we are to understand the discipline of God in particular, we must seek to understand what it accomplishes. His Word gives us many wonderful reasons for why we are disciplined:

- We are disciplined by God so that we may have rest in the day of trouble. (Psalm 94:12-13)
- We are disciplined by God because he loves us and he delights in us. (Proverbs 3:11-12)
- We are disciplined by God as a means of bringing us back to him. (Hosea 6:1)
- We are disciplined by God so that we may not be condemned along with the world. (1 Corinthians 11:32)
- We are disciplined by God for our good, that we may share

in his holiness. (Hebrews 12:10)
- We are disciplined by God so that it trains us to yield a peaceful fruit of righteousness in our lives. (Hebrews 12:11)

As you read over these, ponder your life. Have you seen God's discipline at work? Was it pleasant? How were you transformed as a result of discipline?

Although the Bible makes a clear case for the benefits of God's discipline, often it is difficult for us to believe. The author of Hebrews tells us, "all discipline seems painful rather than pleasant" (Hebrews 12:11). In the midst of God's discipline, we may not have the ability to see beyond that moment for many years, or perhaps an entire lifetime.

The reality is that discipline is painful, and we don't want pain. Although God reminds us it is for our good, we would rather avoid it. We fear the pain of discipline, and our fear quickly sours when we begin to doubt God's goodness. Even when God says, "It's because I love you," we are quick to think that God is hurting us because he does not truly care for us. We may grow bitter toward God for his attempts at refining us and producing righteousness in our lives. It is possible to go into a season of the Lord's discipline and come out with a hardened heart. Trust me when I tell you this is a terrible path.

If discipline is not just for the purpose of pain, what is its purpose? The simplest answer is that God disciplines us when our lives don't look like Christ. Although the following passage does not explicitly mention discipline, it has influenced how I understand God's discipline in my life:

> And we know that for those who love God all things work together for good, for those who are called ac-

cording to his purpose. For those whom he foreknew he also predestined to be conformed to the image of his Son, in order that he might be the firstborn among many brothers. (Romans 8:28-29)

I would imagine that many of my readers are familiar with the first half of this passage. Romans 8:28 is a well-known verse. Verse 29, however, provides important context. I believe these two verses are meant to be read together as the same thought.

Romans 8:28 tells us that for those who love God (i.e. Christians), God is working all things for good. It is important to pause here and note that *God's discipline falls under the category of "all things"*. In this sense, discipline is within the scope of the passage.

Notice the verse doesn't say "their good". It just says "good". Well, what is that good? What is the purpose that we are called to as his children?

Verse 29 answers that for us. From the Father's perspective, his good in our lives and his purpose for our lives is to be conformed to the image of Jesus - his only begotten Son. This realization shattered my worldview. It means the circumstances that I once viewed as bad are now opportunities for God's good purpose to have its way in my life.

God's good purpose may look like sickness if that's what it takes to make me more like Jesus. God's good purpose may look like loneliness if that's what it takes to make me more like Jesus. God's good purpose may look like poverty if that's what it takes to make me more like Jesus. God's good purpose may look like the loss of a loved one if that's what it takes to make me more like Jesus.

Christlikeness is the driving force behind our Father's discipline and sanctification. He may humble you, take everything from you, and expose all your hidden sins to the world in order to make you more like Christ. God loves you too much to leave you undisciplined. Bearing the image of Christ is the good purpose of the Father for his children, and he will do anything he can to bring our image-bearing to full maturity.

To be clear, not all suffering is God's discipline. This is very important. If we view all our suffering in this life as a result of God's discipline, we may develop a distorted view of God. We must show discernment. God does indeed discipline us and conform us to the image of Jesus, but there may be other causes for the trials we face as well.

For example, we live in a broken and sinful world. Until Christ returns and makes everything new, the creation we see is hurting and deteriorating. We sometimes experience this brokenness up close due to simply existing in a fallen world. Another example would be persecution. God disciplines us when we are *not* living like Christ, but we experience persecution from the world when we *are* living like Christ. Although my focus here is discipline, bear in mind that not all suffering is God's discipline.

Let us return to the why: Why does the Father discipline his children? In short, God disciplines us according to his good purpose because he dearly loves us and wants to make us like Christ. If this is the reason why we are disciplined, then there must be a means of discipline. There must be methods by which we can become more like Jesus.

Discipline: The How

When we sin, God rebukes us through discipline. God's discipline is not limited to a specific strategy; however, we do see some themes in Scripture for what the discipline of God looks like. We will cover four means that God uses to discipline his children: Idol removal, natural consequences, the Church, and Satan. We will examine each of these in turn.

> When you discipline a man with rebukes for sin, you consume like a moth what is dear to him; surely all mankind is a mere breath! *Selah* (Psalm 39:11)

This verse presents a very raw truth about how God disciplines. It may involve removing idols. I remember telling someone in college, "I can't trust God with my health." Not many years after that, God allowed me to have muscle and nerve issues which caused me to trust in him rather than in my health. What do you idolize?

If - like I did - you idolize health, God may allow ailments or injuries. If you idolize your money or possessions, God may forcefully remove them. If you idolize relationships, God may keep you from them. If you idolize your own success, God may allow you to fail. While these losses and hardships are *not always* indicators of sin in your life, they are all opportunities to check your heart. These scenarios are how God, in his grace, may choose to discipline you for your idol worship. The Lord will consume what is dearest to you until he is all that is dear to you. So the questions must be asked: What is dearest to you? Does it captivate your heart more than Jesus?

If so, then take heed: Turn your heart back to God and away

from sin. According to his Word, he will consume the things that you thought were worth sinning over. Charles Spurgeon once said, "Do not drive your heavenly Father to hard measures. If He means to bless you he will not let you go unpunished; but he will smite you with heavy strokes."[45]

These heavy strokes may often look like natural consequences. This is another means of God's discipline. If you treat your body in a way that is not honoring to God, or if you treat people in a way that is unloving, or if you do not submit to the authorities God has placed over you, there will often be an unpleasant result. Here are some examples: Sex outside of God's design may produce disease. Gossiping about someone could result in loss of friendship. Driving over the speed limit earns you a speeding ticket from the authorities (see Romans 13:1-7). The point is that when we experience the effects of our sin, it should cause us to consider the state of our hearts. The natural consequences of our actions may very well be God disciplining us for our sin.

God will also use his Church to discipline his children. The Church is God's kingdom on earth, his bride, and his body. The Church is the faith-based community of believers. Within the context of a local church; there is fellowship, structured leadership, and orderly worship. Ideally, every Christian is involved in their local church community.

If there is a case where a believer is caught in a sin, the church should be the first line of discipline. It can take several forms. It may look like gentle correction from another believer:

> Brothers, if anyone is caught in any transgression, you who are spiritual should restore him in a spirit of gentleness. Keep watch on yourself, lest you too be

tempted.
(Galatians 6:1)

The preferred outcome of church discipline is always restoration, forgiveness, and triumph over sin. That being said, there is another outcome for a repeated and unrepentant lifestyle of sin:

> If your brother sins against you, go and tell him his fault, between you and him alone. If he listens to you, you have gained your brother. But if he does not listen, take one or two others along with you, that every charge may be established by the evidence of two or three witnesses. If he refuses to listen to them, tell it to the church. And if he refuses to listen even to the church, let him be to you as a Gentile and a tax collector.
> (Matthew 18:15-17)

Jesus spoke these words to a Jewish audience. At this time and in this culture, Jews did not associate with Gentiles because they were thought to be unclean, or with tax collectors because they were thought to be traitors. Jesus is saying that if someone is charged with a repeated sin and will not listen to the loving rebuke of the church, that person should be excommunicated. This may seem harsh, until you realize that the Church is to be different from the world; holy. We are to imitate Jesus Christ the righteous — the light of the world. Paul once wrote, "For what partnership has righteousness with lawlessness? Or what fellowship has light with darkness?" (2 Corinthians 6:14). These questions are rhetorical. The answer is *none*.

This brings up an important point: You as a Christian can be a means of your Father's loving discipline to your brothers and sisters in Christ. If you see a dear brother or sister in the Lord falling into sin, admonish them in gentleness and love. Conversely, if another believer approaches you about sin in your life, humble yourself and listen very closely.

Scripture makes it clear that discipline of repeated sin must involve the community of the church. In a letter to Timothy, Paul wrote, "As for those who persist in sin, rebuke them in the presence of all, so that the rest may stand in fear" (1 Timothy 5:20). This sort of action within the church is very purposeful. It produces greater accountability within the church body, and it communicates the severity of living in sin. The fear of public rebuke acts as a deterrent to sin for every member of the church body.

We must bring more Scripture into the scope of this topic. Within the early Corinthian church, there was a man who was found to be in an ongoing sexual relationship with his stepmother. Paul addressed this issue in his letter to the Corinthians and gave instruction on discipline:

> When you are assembled in the name of the Lord Jesus and my spirit is present, with the power of our Lord Jesus, you are to deliver this man to Satan for the destruction of the flesh, so that his spirit may be saved in the day of the Lord. (1 Corinthians 5:4-5)

Many commentators seem to think the phrase "deliver this man to Satan" means to excommunicate this man from the church. This is thought to be the case because a couple verses earlier in 1 Corinthians 5:2 Paul said that the man should be "removed from among" them. In addition, within the Church, Christ is King; outside of the church, Satan is the temporary "ruler of this world" (John 12:31). In sending the man into the domain of Satan, the hope is that the man will reach a heart of repentance and his soul is saved, even if it means he bears the consequences of his sin in this life.

The phrase "deliver this man to Satan" could mean the church assembly is praying that God would use Satan as a means of bringing about repentance and salvation in the man's life. Paul records a similar form of correction in his letter to Timothy:

> Some have made shipwreck of their faith, among whom are Hymenaeus and Alexander, whom I have handed over to Satan that they may learn not to blaspheme.
> (1 Timothy 1:19b-20)

This passage transitions us into one last method of discipline from God that we will review: God the Father may use Satan to discipline his children.

This may come as a shock. Isn't Satan opposed to God's will? Yes, he is. But Satan must always conform to God's will. God keeps Satan on a tight leash. Satan can do nothing to us unless God permits it. God may employ Satan to sanctify his people.

An easy way to understand this concept is to consider the Jewish people in the Old Testament. When they turned away from God, God used foreign nations - evil nations - to judge his people and bring about his will. These foreign nations that rejected God were instruments in his hand.

When God's people worshiped other gods, they were invaded, plundered, and taken captive by foreign kingdoms around them. This happened repeatedly until it culminated in Assyria conquering Israel and Babylon conquering Judah.

In the same way that God used these wicked kingdoms to draw his people back to him, he can use Satan to draw your heart back to him. God can employ Satan – the prideful angel who fell from heaven – to rid you of your own pride. God can make use of Satan – the father of lies – in order to rid you of your own lies and secrecy.

That being said, God and Satan are not *yin* and *yang*. There is not an eternal conflict between the equal powers of light and dark, with God and Satan on either side. God *dominates* Satan (Revelation 12:10). It's not even a contest. Jesus reigns supreme and unchallenged. Satan and his demons are powerless in the hands of the Lord. God will do with them as he pleases.

A biblical example of God using Satan for discipline can be found in the life of Paul. In 2 Corinthians 12, Paul writes that God had given him visions and revelations. These visions are not described in detail, but here is what Paul has to say after mentioning them:

> So to keep me from becoming conceited because of the surpassing greatness of the revelations, a thorn was given me in the flesh, a messenger of Satan to harass me, to keep me from becoming conceited.
> (2 Corinthians 12:7)

It is unclear what this thorn in the flesh was in Paul's life. I would imagine that it was some sort of physical ailment or trial. Whatever it was, the thorn in the flesh was a messenger of Satan, and it harassed Paul to keep him from boasting and help him to rely on God's all-sufficient grace. What do you think God would do in your life to remove your pride and cause you to rely on him?

As we have examined our Father's many means of discipline, I hope that you have seen his love for you shine through. Your heavenly Father may remove idols in your life because he desires your affection to be for him alone. He may allow you to reap the natural results of your actions so that you are warned in where sin will take you. The Church is provided as a loving community to put up guardrails and keep us on a path of holiness. Even our accuser Satan is a pawn in the hand of God to push us toward total reliance on the One who calls us beloved children.

***

Beloved child of God, the fact that your heavenly Father will do anything and everything to bring you to repentance and make you more like Jesus should cause you to fear and tremble. This knowledge should cause you to change your ways and to repent. God *will* discipline you for your sin. John Bunyan emphasizes this point:

> If you are an adopted child of God and you sin, God will save your soul. But he will make you know that sin is sin. If necessary he will discipline you with a rod made of scorpions. Read all the book of Lamentations. Read the complaints of Job and David. Read what happened to God's Son, his beloved, when he stood in the place of sinners. Jesus was completely innocent, but you, oh sinning child of God are not. God is not unjust

to discipline you. It is necessary that you should be
disciplined for your sin.[46]

I think John Bunyan hit the nail on the head with this statement. Although your soul is saved, God must still discipline you for your sin. So what have we learned in this chapter?

The Father disciplines us because he loves us. Healthy fear of God's discipline means that we revere God more than we fear the pain of discipline. A healthy fear of God requires a deep understanding of our identity as beloved and adopted children. He is now our Father through faith in Jesus. Our heavenly Father is a good Father and the best Father. He invites us into his loving embrace.

As our Father, he must discipline us as his children. He disciplines us because he delights in us and he wants us to be holy and righteous. Most importantly, he disciplines us because he wants us to be like his Son Jesus.

God has many methods by which he may choose to discipline us. If our hearts treasure something more than God, he may remove it. If we worship idols instead of Jesus, he will knock them down. The Lord will consume what is dearest to us until he is all that is dear to us. Even when we experience the natural consequences of our sin, we should seek to understand what God wants us to learn. God may even use church discipline or Satan in order to discipline us.

I hope this knowledge is as transformational in your life as it has been in mine. I hope that as you experience God's discipline, you won't run and hide from the pain. I pray that the discomfort of the Lord's chastisement draws you closer to him. I want you to be able to ask yourself, "Is this worth it?" and answer with a resounding "*YES*".

If you are in a season right now where God is disciplining you, please do not harden your heart toward him. Revere him as your loving Father. Stay tender toward him and allow him to conform you to the image of Christ.

If you find yourself being enticed by sin or habitually giving into sin, be warned. God will surely intervene. Choose to revere your Father and follow in the footsteps of his Son. Fear his discipline and turn away from evil.

Although God disciplines his children who sin, he also shows compassion on his children who fear him:

> As a father shows compassion to his children, so the LORD shows compassion to those who fear him. (Psalm 103:13)

If you have a healthy fear of the Father's discipline — revering God first and fearing the pain of discipline second — you will turn away from sin and you can be sure that God will show compassion to you as his child. If you do not have healthy fear and instead choose to hide in sin, then God will discipline you as his beloved child to bring you back to himself.

Your Father is for you either way.

9

The Big Picture

My wife has a knack for solving jigsaw puzzles. I never even attempted a puzzle before we met, but in the last couple years we have completed three jigsaw puzzles together. We started off with a 300 piece puzzle, then moved up to a 500 piece and finally a 1000 piece. Solving these puzzles took some time! Working together to complete the pictures has been an enjoyable way to spend time with one another.

Oftentimes, it is difficult to see the big picture when you're only staring at one piece of the puzzle. The puzzle piece might contain a small detail from the larger picture, or it could be a solid color piece of a larger object in the canvas. Each piece must be carefully evaluated, grouped with like pieces and - with careful study of its connections - joined to its rightful place. The more pieces are in place, the easier it becomes to identify the correct positions for other puzzle pieces. Until each unique puzzle piece is accounted for and placed in its correct location, you won't be able to enjoy the picture as a whole.

As we have seen over the last eight chapters, there are many different aspects of fearing God. Each of these pieces carry significance and reveal more of who God is and how we can have a proper fear of him. By filling each space with biblical truth about the fear of the Lord, our picture grows more and more complete. As we continue to seek God through his Word and grow in spiritual maturity, God will continually expand our puzzle, graciously giving us more pieces of the puzzle to knowing him, loving him, and fearing him.

With this image in mind, let's gather the puzzle pieces we have been carefully examining and take a look at the beautiful picture they build as they join together.

The groundwork of this endeavor requires us to find the edge pieces first. As humans, we must identify the objects that we are prone to fear. Generic fear tells us to fear things other than God, yet fearing God rightly is crucial to our lives if we want to honor him and prosper. This principle is clearly laid out in the Bible. Since God's Word has much to say on the subject, I put forth a definition of "fear of the Lord" as follows:

> *A proper fear of the Lord is a personal response to being in awe of God's greatness; or being convicted by God's chastisement, in which someone is led by the Holy Spirit to know God and love him in a deeper way than before; resulting in gained wisdom, blessings, joy, reverence for God, and obedience to God.*

With the idea of how we ought to fear God made plain, we discover that there is more to fearing God than we thought. We have more pieces to fill in. In fact, how we fear God will fall inside a quadrant of four fears: greatness and chastisement; healthy or unhealthy.

Based on how we are experiencing God, we will either fear his greatness or his chastisement. The primary way we can fear God's greatness is to be in awe of him. God is awesome because of his holiness, creation, power, and deeds.

Shifting our gaze to God's chastisement, we know that God will rightly judge sin. This truth is sobering, and it should motivate us to share the Good News of Jesus with those who are still under the wrath of God.

Furthermore, our fear may evoke a healthy or unhealthy response. If our fear of God causes us to draw near to him in love, humility, and obedience; then it is healthy. Conversely, an unhealthy fear causes us to respond toward God in anger and shame. Instead of seeking a relationship with God, we reject him and remain distant.

The clarity of these four fears enables us to examine the object of our fear, God, in closer detail. We are now ready to fill in the middle pieces. It is time to examine how the fear of the Lord relates to the Trinity.

The glory of Jesus beckons us to fear him because of his authority as the Righteous Judge, the Word of God, the worker of miracles and the forgiver of sins. A study of the Holy Spirit reminds us of his vital role in leading us into healthy fear of the Lord. His presence gives us the mind of Christ, empowers us with resurrection life, and grants us divine fear that draws us closer to God the Father. When we behold God the Father as his beloved children, we come to know that his loving discipline is meant to evoke a fearful reverence of him. The purpose of this discipline is to conform us to the image of Christ and keep us from sin.

The Bible presents us with a beautiful and complete picture of fearing God. I have tried to encapsulate many of these truths within this book. It would be a tragedy if you finished this chapter, closed the book, and remained unaffected by the truths presented here. We should all desire to take the biblical knowledge in our heads and allow it to change our hearts. By God's grace, the fear of the Lord has brought about this sort of change in my life.

* * *

When I was young, I watched the Jesus Film[47] and was deeply moved to see a visual depiction of Jesus dying for my sins. It was Jesus' love for me on the cross and the healthy fear of God's judgment on sin that made me realize I needed Jesus as my Savior. I understood that Jesus took God's wrath that I deserved upon himself and offered me the gift of forgiveness and eternal life. What else could I do but trust in him for my salvation? I decided to get baptized as a public profession of faith.

But what is faith without obedience?

For many years after that, my life was defined by lust, lies, and pride. This brought me to a low point where I was finally confronted with my sin. A healthy fear of the Lord helped me to realize that following God meant I couldn't continue practicing sin. I had to surrender every part of me to God and stop walking down a path of destruction.

Rather than just professing my faith and appearing to be a Christ-follower, I had to truly follow him with all my heart, soul, mind, and strength. Living a double-life wasn't an option. The fear of the Lord brought me to a place of conviction and greater desire to say yes to him and no to myself. It also led me to being open and honest with my Christian community. Jesus was now the Lord of my life. By his grace, I was truly saved and in a relationship with him.

But sanctification is a process.

A few years ago, I found myself living an indulgent lifestyle. My evenings and weekends were consumed with playing video games. I spent thousands of hours and dollars on online gaming thinking that somehow it would satisfy me. During the process of pursuing my girlfriend (who is now my wife), I realized that our relationship would not be God-honoring if I were prioritizing entertainment over God and over her. Beyond my dating relationship, I couldn't serve my local church well while finding my identity in video games.

The fear of the Lord gave me wisdom and empowered me to make the change required. Although it felt painful, I deleted all my online gaming accounts and obliterated thousands of dollars of games and in-game items in the process. Gaming was causing me to sin, and I had to cut it off.

In this particular instance, God used a story in the book of Acts to convict me. In Acts 19:17-20, it describes Christians in the city of Ephesus coming together and confessing their sins. Not only was there confession, but some prior pagan magicians burned up all their magic books - totaling in millions of dollars today.

The text says they did this because the fear of God had fallen upon them. I look at this as a prime example of healthy fear of the Lord. Fearing God should bring about this sort of zeal, earnestness, and drastic change when you truly understand who you fear and how he loves you. I have experienced this transformation firsthand.

Healthy fear of the Lord is not just an occasional response to conviction. It is very much at work in my life on a daily basis. One of the first things I do in the morning is go to God in prayer and meditate on his words in the Bible. I want to please my

Father, yet I know I am prone to sin, so in desperation I turn to him for grace and strength. The fear of the Lord has caused my heart to echo the words of Simon Peter in John 6:68, "Lord, to whom shall we go? You have the words of eternal life." The fear of God has kept me close to his Word. This is not to say that I always have perfect and consistent quiet times. My flesh is still prone to wander, but God's love and a healthy fear of him continually pulls me back in.

* * *

At this point you might be thinking to yourself, "That's great for you, but I just don't know where to start. I need practical steps. How can I grow in my healthy fear of the Lord?" I have good news for you: By reading this book, you have already taken a step in the right direction. That being said, I do want to leave you with points of application. It is vital that we apply the truths about fearing God to our lives.

When I think of application, I think of *The Joy of Fearing God* by Jerry Bridges. It is an excellent book that I have already quoted twice. If you want to read a book on fearing God written by someone with decades of experience and lifelong service to Christ, Jerry's book would be a great resource. In chapter 8 of his book, he gives six practical steps on how to grow in the fear of God. I have summarized them here in a list:

1. Ask God for an undivided heart to fear him.
2. Consistently expose your heart and mind to God's Word.
3. Study the Bible in-depth.
4. Supplement your Scripture intake with good books that grow your fear of God.

5. Train yourself to think great thoughts about God on a daily basis.
6. Get a friend who will hold you accountable and encourage you in the fear of the Lord.[48]

If I were to comment on this list that Bridges has compiled, I would clarify two things. First, I would add that fear of the Lord is impossible without knowing him. You must first have a relationship with him and furthermore spend time investing in that relationship through prayer. Whether it is using the ACTS prayer model[49], or keeping a prayer journal, or reminders on your phone; communicating with God is non-negotiable if you want to know and fear him.

Second, center your thoughts on Jesus Christ. This is related to Bridges' step 5 - "Think great thoughts about God." Whenever I am not feeling close to God, or whenever I am neglecting to fear him and obey him, the remedy is to dwell on Jesus and his love. Choose to think about the life, death, resurrection, and intercession of Jesus. This will always prime your heart to fear him with love, awe, and reverence.

The pages of Bible verses in the appendices speak to the benefits of fearing God. If you turn to them, it will not take you long to pick up on several key themes: The fear of God brings wisdom and knowledge. The fear of God protects one from sin, evil, and injustice. The fear of God changes one's heart to delight in God. The fear of God brings about many blessings as one surrenders to God and obeys him. The fear of God leads to eternal life. These are but a fraction of the truths you will find.

Everything we have covered is not meant to end here. This book is designed to be a springboard for you to know God and grow in a healthy fear of him. My earnest prayer is that you would be encouraged by the truths laid out in these pages. Know that the fear of the Lord is biblical. Understand that the fear of the Lord is beautiful. As you feast on his Word, may you be filled with healthy fear that brings you closer to God.

Be *Fear Full*.

Acknowledgments

I am beyond humbled that God laid this project on my heart. Without the Lord's guidance and grace, I would not have been able to accomplish this work. I am tremendously thankful for Christ's work in my life and his mercy. He is so good.

My deepest gratitude goes out to my wife Hannah who has stuck by me and supported me like no other. She is an incredible helper in so many ways; including this book endeavor. Her intelligence and knowledge of the Bible have been extremely insightful. She has also done some editing on *Fear Full*! I love you Hannah!

I want give a huge thank you to my sister Rebekah. She did an incredible job on designing the cover for this book. She was very patient with me as I critiqued her designs. I am very blessed by her artistic abilities.

I am honored to have a church family that has been so excited about this book project and has encouraged me and challenged me to stay the course. Whether it's my Bible study group, the praise team, or my pastors; I am sharpened by the community surrounding me at my church.

I am also very privileged to have my parents Bart and Danielle, as well as other family members who have all been huge supporters of me for my entire life. In addition, my extended family has enabled me in so many ways to serve God and follow his leading. I'm extremely blessed by all the theological conversations I've been able to have with my parents-in-law, Lentz and Amy Upshaw. Thank you for your kindness and prayers!

I'm grateful for my experience volunteering with Doxazo Ministries. The opportunity to disciple high school students was a huge reason why I started looking into the topic of fearing the Lord.

I want to thank my friends Christopher Bazell, Jared Schoeneberg, Steven Davis, and Kendall Dwyre for all giving me space to verbally process the concepts found in this book. I also want to thank my friend and mentor Dave Clauson for giving me helpful pointers for writing and organizing my thoughts.

Finally, I want to thank the online writing service Reedsy for the template and the web design to make my writing very intuitive and structured.

Soli Deo Gloria!

Appendix A: "Fear of the Lord" Bible Verse Commentary

27 Verses Total:

2 Chronicles 14:14

And they attacked all the cities around Gerar, for the fear of the Lord was upon them. They plundered all the cities, for there was much plunder in them.

What does this verse say about fear of the Lord?

King Asa and his Judean army were relying on God to give them a miraculous military victory against the Ethiopians. Although Judah was greatly outnumbered, God was with them to defeat the Ethiopians. The surrounding pagan cities were also attacked by Judah along the way, and all the inhabitants feared the Lord because they saw how he had strengthened Judah in battle.

* * *

2 Chronicles 17:10

And the fear of the Lord fell upon all the kingdoms of the

lands that were around Judah, and they made no war against Jehoshaphat.

What does this verse say about fear of the Lord?
When Jehoshaphat became king of Judah, he fortified his cities, removed idols, was courageous to follow God's commandments, and ensured that God's laws were taught throughout Judah. As a result, the surrounding nations feared God so that they did not attack Judah, and instead felt compelled to bring tribute to Jehoshaphat.

* * *

2 Chronicles 19:7
Now then, let the fear of the Lord be upon you. Be careful what you do, for there is no injustice with the Lord our God, or partiality or taking bribes.

What does this verse say about fear of the Lord?
These instructions are given by King Jehoshaphat to the judges he appointed in his cities. The fear of the Lord was to motivate justice, impartiality, and honesty in their dealings.

* * *

2 Chronicles 19:9
And he charged them: "Thus you shall do in the fear of the Lord, in faithfulness, and with your whole heart"

What does this verse say about fear of the Lord?
In addition to judges, Jehoshaphat appointed men in

Jerusalem who would decide disputed cases that arose in the cities of Judah. They were charged to fulfill their duties out of the fear of the Lord and to faithfully speak warnings when necessary. Otherwise, they would be guilty before God for neglecting their duty.

* * *

Job 28:28

And he said to man, 'Behold, the fear of the Lord, that is wisdom, and to turn away from evil is understanding.' "

What does this verse say about fear of the Lord?

The fear of the Lord is synonymous with wisdom. If you are wise, you fear the Lord. If you fear the Lord, you are wise. In this verse, fear of the Lord also correlates with turning away from anything evil.

* * *

Psalm 19:9

the fear of the Lord is clean, enduring forever;
the rules of the Lord are true, and righteous altogether.

What does this verse say about fear of the Lord?

The Hebrew word for clean here means "ceremonially and morally pure." This indicates that the fear of the Lord is associated with the highest standards of purity according to God's law. Furthermore, the fear of the Lord endures forever. It will never cease to exist.

***

Psalm 34:11
Come, O children, listen to me;
I will teach you the fear of the LORD.

What does this verse say about fear of the Lord?
This implies that the fear of the Lord is something that can be learned and taught. In addition, the subsequent verses in Psalm 34 indicate that fear of the Lord is related to having speech that is honest and good; pursuing peace and rejecting evil.

***

Psalm 111:10
The fear of the LORD is the beginning of wisdom;
all those who practice it have a good understanding.
His praise endures forever!

What does this verse say about fear of the Lord?
The fear of the Lord will set a person on the path of gaining true wisdom. The fear of the Lord is something that should be lived out and practiced. Acting in the fear of the Lord results in deeper understanding.

***

Proverbs 1:7
The fear of the LORD is the beginning of knowledge; fools despise wisdom and instruction.

What does this verse say about fear of the Lord?

Closely related to wisdom, the fear of the Lord will also set a person on the path of gaining true knowledge. To oppose wisdom and learning shows foolishness and a lack of the fear of the Lord.

* * *

Proverbs 1:29

Because they hated knowledge
and did not choose the fear of the LORD

What does this verse say about fear of the Lord?

The context in Proverbs 1 which surrounds this verse shows that choosing to reject wisdom and the fear of the Lord brings rebellion, complacency, and destruction.

* * *

Proverbs 2:5

then you will understand the fear of the LORD
and find the knowledge of God.

What does this verse say about fear of the Lord?

This verse describes the result of seeking wisdom. The verses before this (Proverbs 2:1-4) inform us that the fear of the Lord is understood by a person who listens to wise instruction and searches diligently for insight.

* * *

Proverbs 8:13

The fear of the LORD is hatred of evil.
Pride and arrogance and the way of evil
and perverted speech I hate.

What does this verse say about fear of the Lord?

In this verse, the fear of the Lord is equated with hating evil. Pride, arrogance, and perverted speech are associated with the evil. A person will naturally hate this evil if they have fear of the Lord.

* * *

Proverbs 9:10

The fear of the LORD is the beginning of wisdom,
and the knowledge of the Holy One is insight.

What does this verse say about fear of the Lord?

This verse's parallel structure compares fear of the Lord to knowledge of the Holy One. The result will be gained wisdom and insight.

* * *

Proverbs 10:27

The fear of the LORD prolongs life,
but the years of the wicked will be short.

What does this verse say about fear of the Lord?

This verse contrasts the fear of the Lord with wickedness. The fear of the Lord leads to life while wickedness leads to death. This concept can be applied as a general principle to physical life/death, but it also speaks to an even more sure reality regarding eternal life/death.

* * *

Proverbs 14:26

In the fear of the LORD one has strong confidence, and his children will have a refuge.

What does this verse say about fear of the Lord?

The fear of the Lord produces a mighty confidence in the Lord. This confidence and trust in God as one's refuge will strengthen their family as well.

* * *

Proverbs 14:27

The fear of the LORD is a fountain of life,
that one may turn away from the snares of death.

What does this verse say about fear of the Lord?

The fear of the Lord is like finding life-giving water. Jesus himself says that he is the source of living water (John 4:10-14). The presence of water enables a person to choose life and not die of thirst. Similarly, without the refreshment that the fear of the Lord brings, they will become trapped by sin and death.

* * *

Proverbs 15:16

Better is a little with the fear of the LORD
than great treasure and trouble with it.

What does this verse say about fear of the Lord?
The fear of the Lord is more valuable than material wealth.

* * *

Proverbs 15:33
The fear of the LORD is instruction in wisdom,
and humility comes before honor.

What does this verse say about fear of the Lord?
The fear of the Lord is a teacher. It teaches wisdom to those who will listen. Also implied here is the idea that humility is closely related to fear of the Lord. Thus, wisdom and honor are the result of humility and the fear of the Lord.

* * *

Proverbs 16:6
By steadfast love and faithfulness iniquity is atoned for, and by the fear of the LORD one turns away from evil.

What does this verse say about fear of the Lord?
The fear of the Lord is the means by which a person resists evil.

* * *

Proverbs 19:23

> The fear of the LORD leads to life,
> and whoever has it rests satisfied;
> he will not be visited by harm.

What does this verse say about fear of the Lord?

The principle here is that fear of the Lord sets one on a path to a secure, restful, and satisfied life.

* * *

Proverbs 22:4

> The reward for humility and fear of the LORD
> is riches and honor and life.

What does this verse say about fear of the Lord?

The fear of the Lord must be paired with humility. This combination may result in riches, honor, and life. Most importantly – heavenly riches, spiritual honor, and eternal life.

* * *

Proverbs 23:17

> Let not your heart envy sinners,
> but continue in the fear of the LORD all the day.

What does this verse say about fear of the Lord?

Constant fear of the Lord is encouraged as a healthy alternative to envy.

* * *

Isaiah 11:2

And the Spirit of the LORD shall rest upon him, the Spirit of wisdom and understanding, the Spirit of counsel and might, the Spirit of knowledge and the fear of the LORD.

What does this verse say about fear of the Lord?

This verse is a prophecy about Jesus that was fulfilled when Jesus was baptized by his cousin John and the Spirit descended on him like a dove (Matthew 3:16, Mark 1:10, Luke 3:22, John 1:32). This Spirit of the Lord – the Holy Spirit – is characterized by divine fear of the Lord; as well as wisdom, understanding, counsel, might, and knowledge. This is the Spirit that resides in every Christian.

* * *

Isaiah 11:3

And his delight shall be in the fear of the LORD. He shall not judge by what his eyes see, or decide disputes by what his ears hear

What does this verse say about fear of the Lord?

This verse is also a prophecy about Jesus. Jesus delights in the fear of the Lord. This was made evident by Jesus' life on earth. While on earth, Jesus showed that he had reverence for his Father in heaven and obeyed all that the Father willed.

* * *

Isaiah 33:6

and he will be the stability of your times,

abundance of salvation, wisdom, and knowledge;
the fear of the LORD is Zion's treasure.

What does this verse say about fear of the Lord?

"He" in this verse is referring to God himself. The word Zion refers to the dwelling place of God's people, or the Kingdom of God. In God's kingdom, the fear of him is to be highly valued.

* * *

Acts 9:31

So the church throughout all Judea and Galilee and Samaria had peace and was being built up. And walking in the fear of the Lord and in the comfort of the Holy Spirit, it multiplied.

What does this verse say about fear of the Lord?

This verse succeeds the narrative of Saul becoming a Christian - therefore ceasing his persecution - and beginning to preach the Gospel in public. The growth of the early church is connected to how they feared the Lord and were comforted by the Holy Spirit.

* * *

2 Corinthians 5:11

Therefore, knowing the fear of the Lord, we persuade others. But what we are is known to God, and I hope it is known also to your conscience.

What does this verse say about fear of the Lord?

The previous verse 10 mentions the judgment seat of Christ

which all will face after death. Knowledge of the fear of the Lord as it relates to eternal judgment should motivate Christians to live holy lives and persuade people to be reconciled to God through faith in Jesus before facing judgment.

Appendix B: "Fear God" Bible Verse Commentary

15 Verses Total:

Genesis 22:12
He said, "Do not lay your hand on the boy or do anything to him, for now I know that you fear God, seeing you have not withheld your son, your only son, from me."

What does this verse say about fearing God?
This is when God was testing Abraham by asking him to sacrifice his son Isaac. Fearing God involves not withholding anything from God; including the things that are most dear to us.

* * *

Genesis 42:18
On the third day Joseph said to them, "Do this and you will live, for I fear God:"

What does this verse say about fearing God?

Where this verse picks up, Joseph has just imprisoned his brothers for three days. He is testing them to see if they've changed (after they sold him into slavery many years ago), and they don't yet recognize him. They may assume that he is a worshiper of foreign gods, but Joseph is making it clear that his actions are motivated by the fear of God.

* * *

Exodus 18:21

Moreover, look for able men from all the people, men who fear God, who are trustworthy and hate a bribe, and place such men over the people as chiefs of thousands, of hundreds, of fifties, and of tens.

What does this verse say about fearing God?

Moses' father-in-law is giving Moses advice on how to govern the people of Israel. He equates men who fear God with those who are trustworthy and hate bribes. These are the desired qualities of those who are to judge cases between the people. Fearing God involves being trustworthy.

* * *

Deuteronomy 25:18

how he attacked you on the way when you were faint and weary, and cut off your tail, those who were lagging behind you, and he did not fear God.

What does this verse say about fearing God?

This is referencing Exodus 17:8-16 when Amalek came and

fought with the Israelites. A lack of fearing God is connected with attacking God's chosen people. The resulting command to Israel was to completely destroy the Amalekites.

* * *

Job 1:9

Then Satan answered the LORD and said, "Does Job fear God for no reason?"

What does this verse say about fearing God?
Satan is coming before God and accusing the man Job of only fearing God because God had blessed him. By the end of Job's story, we know that he did fear God regardless of his circumstances. We should also fear God regardless of circumstance.

* * *

Psalm 55:19

God will give ear and humble them,
he who is enthroned from of old, *Selah*
because they do not change
and do not fear God.

What does this verse say about fearing God?
God forcefully humbles those who do not fear him.

* * *

Psalm 66:16

Come and hear, all you who fear God,
and I will tell what he has done for my soul.

What does this verse say about fearing God?
The Psalmist is seeking out those who fear God to share with them what God has done in his life.

* * *

Ecclesiastes 8:12
Though a sinner does evil a hundred times and prolongs his life, yet I know that it will be well with those who fear God, because they fear before him.

What does this verse say about fearing God?
Even if it appears that those who are wicked and evil benefit from their sins, it is a facade. There is greater benefit to be found in fearing God.

* * *

Ecclesiastes 12:13
The end of the matter; all has been heard. Fear God and keep his commandments, for this is the whole duty of man.

What does this verse say about fearing God?
After trying to find meaning in anything possibly good in this life, the writer of Ecclesiastes concludes by saying the only thing in life that matters is fearing God and obeying his commands. Fearing God is the duty of every human being, which means each person is held responsible.

Luke 18:4

For a while he refused, but afterward he said to himself, 'Though I neither fear God nor respect man

What does this verse say about fearing God?

This verse is in a parable that Jesus told. A judge who did not care about justice was described as not fearing God or respecting people. Closely tied to not fearing God is the idea of not showing respect to others and lacking a desire for justice.

* * *

Luke 23:40

But the other rebuked him, saying, "Do you not fear God, since you are under the same sentence of condemnation?"

What does this verse say about fearing God?

This is said by one of the criminals that hung on a cross beside Jesus to the criminal on the other side of Jesus. What the man says here and onward demonstrates that he does fear God. He showed a repentant heart, a recognition of the punishment due his sin, and faith that Jesus could bring him into the kingdom of God. Those who fear God acknowledge their sin and believe in Jesus.

* * *

Acts 13:16

So Paul stood up, and motioning with his hand said: "Men of

Israel and you who fear God, listen.

What does this verse say about fearing God?

This is said when Paul and Barnabas are at Antioch teaching in the Jewish synagogue. He suggests that they have a message not just for the Jews, but for all people who fear God. People from every part of the planet can fear God and respond to the truth about him.

***

Acts 13:26

"Brothers, sons of the family of Abraham, and those among you who fear God, to us has been sent the message of this salvation.

What does this verse say about fearing God?

This verse is also from Paul's speech at Antioch. Here again the message of salvation is addressed to those who fear God.

***

1 Peter 2:17

Honor everyone. Love the brotherhood. Fear God. Honor the emperor.

What does this verse say about fearing God?

At the time this was written, the Roman emperor was probably Nero. Along with loving the church and honoring all people (even those who persecuted Christians like Nero did), Christians are to fear God. Notice that it does not say to fear the emperor.

The implication is that our fear is not for persecutors of the Church. Our fear is reserved only for God.

* * *

Revelation 14:7

And he said with a loud voice, "Fear God and give him glory, because the hour of his judgment has come, and worship him who made heaven and earth, the sea and the springs of water."

What does this verse say about fearing God?

This command is given by an angel. The reason he gives for fearing God is that God's final judgment is coming.

Appendix C: "Fear the Lord" Bible Verse Commentary

32 Verses Total:

Exodus 9:30
"But as for you and your servants, I know that you do not yet fear the LORD God."

What does this verse say about fearing the Lord?
Moses spoke these words to Pharaoh after the seventh plague of Egypt. Pharaoh had acknowledged that he sinned by not letting the Israelites go free. Yet, Moses understood that Pharaoh did not truly repent and fear God. By his subsequent actions, Pharaoh proved Moses' words correct because he still did not obey God's commands.

* * *

Deuteronomy 6:2
that you may fear the LORD your God, you and your son and your son's son, by keeping all his statutes and his commandments, which I command you, all the days of your life, and that

your days may be long.

What does this verse say about fearing the Lord?
Moses is saying these words from God to the people of Israel as he is about to teach them God's law. Fearing the Lord means keeping his laws and obeying his commands. In short, fearing God means doing what he says.

* * *

Deuteronomy 6:24
And the LORD commanded us to do all these statutes, to fear the LORD our God, for our good always, that he might preserve us alive, as we are this day.

What does this verse say about fearing the Lord?
From the same discourse as verse 2 above, Moses reminds the people of Israel that fearing the Lord was for their good.

* * *

Deuteronomy 10:12
"And now, Israel, what does the LORD your God require of you, but to fear the LORD your God, to walk in all his ways, to love him, to serve the LORD your God with all your heart and with all your soul,"

What does this verse say about fearing the Lord?
Again Moses reiterates to the people of Israel that fearing the Lord is required, not optional. They are also required to truly love, obey, and serve God with all of their being.

Deuteronomy 10:20

You shall fear the LORD your God. You shall serve him and hold fast to him, and by his name you shall swear.

What does this verse say about fearing the Lord?

Moses is not shy to repeatedly command Israel to fear the Lord. Related to fearing God, the command here is also to cling to God and to only swear vows by the name of God.

* * *

Deuteronomy 14:23

And before the LORD your God, in the place that he will choose, to make his name dwell there, you shall eat the tithe of your grain, of your wine, and of your oil, and the firstborn of your herd and flock, that you may learn to fear the LORD your God always.

What does this verse say about fearing the Lord?

This command from Moses to Israel is in the context of tithing, but it is more than that. To eat before the Lord was part of the Old Covenant worship and thanksgiving (Leviticus 7:11-18). Fearing the Lord is something that may be learned by giving and worshiping in the Lord's presence.

* * *

Deuteronomy 17:19

And it shall be with him, and he shall read in it all the days of his life, that he may learn to fear the LORD his God by keeping all the words of this law and these statutes, and doing them,

What does this verse say about fearing the Lord?

This section of Moses' instructions to the people of Israel is regarding guidelines for future kings. The king was to have a self-written copy of the law of God to read every day. This instruction was given so that their kings would learn to fear the Lord.

* * *

Deuteronomy 31:12

Assemble the people, men, women, and little ones, and the sojourner within your towns, that they may hear and learn to fear the LORD your God, and be careful to do all the words of this law,

What does this verse say about fearing the Lord?

Here, Moses tells the people to read the Law of God to all Israel every seven years for the Festival of Booths. In hearing the words of the Lord, one learns to fear the Lord.

* * *

Deuteronomy 31:13

and that their children, who have not known it, may hear and learn to fear the LORD your God, as long as you live in the land that you are going over the Jordan to possess.

What does this verse say about fearing the Lord?

This is connected to verse 12 above. Fearing the Lord is important for children as well, not just adults.

* * *

Joshua 4:24

so that all the peoples of the earth may know that the hand of the LORD is mighty, that you may fear the LORD your God forever."

What does this verse say about fearing the Lord?

Immediately after God miraculously dried up the Jordan river to allow Israel to cross, Joshua tells the people to set up a monument of twelve stones on the other side. The purpose of this monument is to remind Israel to fear the Lord, and to remind the nations that God is mighty.

* * *

Joshua 24:14

"Now therefore fear the LORD and serve him in sincerity and in faithfulness. Put away the gods that your fathers served beyond the River and in Egypt, and serve the LORD.

What does this verse say about fearing the Lord?

At the end of Joshua's life, he charged the people of Israel to serve God and fear him. This involved getting rid of anything else that they might be tempted to worship.

* * *

1 Samuel 12:14

If you will fear the LORD and serve him and obey his voice and not rebel against the commandment of the LORD, and if both you and the king who reigns over you will follow the LORD your God, it will be well.

What does this verse say about fearing the Lord?

This is spoken by the prophet and judge Samuel to the people of Israel during his farewell address. After establishing a king for them, Samuel reminds them that fearing God means not living in rebellion to God and that it generally causes a society to thrive.

* * *

1 Samuel 12:24

Only fear the LORD and serve him faithfully with all your heart. For consider what great things he has done for you.

What does this verse say about fearing the Lord?

Later in Samuel's farewell address, he pleads with the people of Israel to fear the Lord and remember what he has done for them. Considering the great things that God has done should produce faithfulness and fear of the Lord.

* * *

2 Kings 17:25

And at the beginning of their dwelling there, they did not fear the LORD. Therefore the LORD sent lions among them, which killed some of them.

What does this verse say about fearing the Lord?

When the king of Assyria brought non-Jews to settle and live in Samaria, they did not know or obey the law of the one true God, and subsequently didn't fear God. The result was disastrous.

* * *

2 Kings 17:28

So one of the priests whom they had carried away from Samaria came and lived in Bethel and taught them how they should fear the LORD.

What does this verse say about fearing the Lord?

Because of the lions killing people, the king of Assyria sent a priest to Samaria to teach the pagan settlers the law of God and how to keep it; in essence, how to fear God. Those who fear God and know the Scriptures can teach others how to understand the Scriptures and fear God.

* * *

2 Kings 17:34

To this day they do according to the former manner. They do not fear the LORD, and they do not follow the statutes or the rules or the law or the commandment that the LORD commanded the children of Jacob, whom he named Israel.

What does this verse say about fearing the Lord?

Although these people in Samaria were taught to obey God's law, they also continued to serve their idols. Serving God and serving false gods is equivalent to not serving God. By definition it violates God's command to have no other gods. Pretending to obey God while still worshiping others shows that a healthy fear of the Lord is absent.

***

2 Kings 17:36

but you shall fear the LORD, who brought you out of the land of Egypt with great power and with an outstretched arm. You shall bow yourselves to him, and to him you shall sacrifice.

What does this verse say about fearing the Lord?

This verse is a reminder of the covenant that the Lord made with Israel which they broke. The people in Israel were to fear God, remember his deliverance, and serve him. Fearing God includes submitting to his authority and being sacrificial toward God.

***

2 Kings 17:39

but you shall fear the LORD your God, and he will deliver you out of the hand of all your enemies."

What does this verse say about fearing the Lord?

Fearing God leads to experiencing his deliverance. In the times of ancient Israel, this meant deliverance from the oppression of other nations.

***

Psalm 15:4
   in whose eyes a vile person is despised,
   but who honors those who fear the LORD;
   who swears to his own hurt and does not change;

What does this verse say about fearing the Lord?
Psalm 15 describes the qualities and actions of a person who may dwell in God's presence. In this verse we see that the person who lives in the presence of God will show honor to those who practice the fear of God.

***

Psalm 22:23
   You who fear the LORD, praise him!
   All you offspring of Jacob, glorify him,
   and stand in awe of him, all you offspring of Israel!

What does this verse say about fearing the Lord?
The one who fears the Lord should praise him.

***

Psalm 33:8
   Let all the earth fear the LORD;
   let all the inhabitants of the world stand in awe of him!

What does this verse say about fearing the Lord?
It is fitting and appropriate for all people to fear the Lord because of his awesomeness.

APPENDIX C: "FEAR THE LORD" BIBLE VERSE COMMENTARY

***

Psalm 34:9
Oh, fear the LORD, you his saints,
for those who fear him have no lack!

What does this verse say about fearing the Lord?
This verse is a call for believers to fear the Lord and a reminder that he provides for those who fear him.

***

Psalm 115:11
You who fear the LORD, trust in the LORD!
He is their help and their shield.

What does this verse say about fearing the Lord?
Someone who fears the Lord trusts him to be their help.

***

Psalm 115:13
he will bless those who fear the LORD,
both the small and the great.

What does this verse say about fearing the Lord?
God indiscriminately blesses those who fear him regardless of earthly status.

***

Psalm 118:4
   Let those who fear the LORD say,
   "His steadfast love endures forever."

What does this verse say about fearing the Lord?
   Those who fear the Lord are able to confidently declare certain qualities about the Lord; such as his steadfast love.

***

Psalm 135:20
   O house of Levi, bless the LORD!
   You who fear the LORD, bless the LORD!

What does this verse say about fearing the Lord?
   The priests of God and all who fear God should bless him with their words and actions.

***

Proverbs 3:7
   Be not wise in your own eyes;
   fear the LORD, and turn away from evil.

What does this verse say about fearing the Lord?
   The act of fearing the Lord involves turning away from things that are evil.

***

Proverbs 24:21

My son, fear the LORD and the king,
and do not join with those who do otherwise,

What does this verse say about fearing the Lord?

This is a father's plea for his son to disassociate from those who do not fear the Lord. It is much wiser to associate with those who fear the Lord.

* * *

Jeremiah 5:24

They do not say in their hearts,
'Let us fear the LORD our God,
who gives the rain in its season,
the autumn rain and the spring rain,
and keeps for us
the weeks appointed for the harvest.'

What does this verse say about fearing the Lord?

Jeremiah the prophet is speaking these words from God to the nation of Judah. The surrounding verses tell us that foolishness, senselessness, stubbornness, rebellion, and wickedness do not lead to fear of the Lord.

* * *

Jeremiah 26:19

Did Hezekiah king of Judah and all Judah put him to death? Did he not fear the LORD and entreat the favor of the LORD, and did not the LORD relent of the disaster that he had pronounced against them? But we are about to bring great disaster upon ourselves."

What does this verse say about fearing the Lord?
The elders of Judah are arguing that putting Jeremiah to death would be a bad idea since Jeremiah is a prophet of God. They are using the case of the prophet Micah as a precedent. The people had listened to Micah's warnings, and so God relented of his punishment. The example from Judah's past was that fearing God and entreating his favor brought deliverance from disaster.

* * *

Hosea 10:3
For now they will say:
"We have no king,
for we do not fear the LORD;
and a king—what could he do for us?"

What does this verse say about fearing the Lord?
Hosea is prophesying against the people of Israel, proclaiming judgment on their idolatry. Due to their wickedness, they will be ruled by another nation instead of by their own king. This is the result of Israel not fearing the Lord.

* * *

Jonah 1:9
And he said to them, "I am a Hebrew, and I fear the LORD, the God of heaven, who made the sea and the dry land."

What does this verse say about fearing the Lord?

Jonah revealed to those he was sailing with that he was a worshiper of the Lord but was currently running away from him. To fear God is to know that he is the Creator of the heavens and the earth and the sea, and that he has authority over all that he has created. The knowledge that Jonah was running away from the all-powerful God rightfully struck fear into the sailors and they worshiped God after seeing his power displayed.

Appendix D: "Fear of God" Bible Verse Commentary

10 Verses Total:

Genesis 20:11

Abraham said, "I did it because I thought, 'There is no fear of God at all in this place, and they will kill me because of my wife.'"

What does this verse say about the fear of God?

In the broader passage, Abraham is explaining to Abimelech why he had lied about Sarah being his wife. Abraham told Sarah to say they were siblings because he thought people would kill him to take his wife Sarah as their own. He assumed that the people living in Gerar did not fear God and concluded that they would not honor life or marriage.

* * *

2 Samuel 23:3

The God of Israel has spoken;
the Rock of Israel has said to me:

When one rules justly over men,
ruling in the fear of God

What does this verse say about the fear of God?

These are some of the last words of King David. He implies that ruling in the fear of God is closely tied to ruling with justice. The verse after this communicates that God shows favor to those who govern in this way.

* * *

2 Chronicles 20:29

And the fear of God came on all the kingdoms of the countries when they heard that the LORD had fought against the enemies of Israel.

What does this verse say about the fear of God?

This is after God caused the Moabites and Ammonites to fight each other instead of fighting against Judah. When stories of God's power travel across kingdoms, the fear of God travels with them.

* * *

2 Chronicles 26:5

He set himself to seek God in the days of Zechariah, who instructed him in the fear of God, and as long as he sought the LORD, God made him prosper.

What does this verse say about the fear of God?

This verse is speaking of King Uzziah. In his case, being

prospered by God is closely tied to seeking after him and being instructed in the fear of the Lord.

* * *

Nehemiah 5:15

The former governors who were before me laid heavy burdens on the people and took from them for their daily ration forty shekels of silver. Even their servants lorded it over the people. But I did not do so, because of the fear of God.

What does this verse say about the fear of God?

These are Nehemiah's words, and this takes place while he is organizing the rebuilding of the walls in Jerusalem. The fear of God compelled him to not extort others.

* * *

Job 4:6

Is not your fear of God your confidence,
and the integrity of your ways your hope?

What does this verse say about the fear of God?

In this verse, one of Job's friends Eliphaz is making the case that the fear of God and integrity will prevent hardships. He speaks presumptuously, however, for Job is an example of the fact that trials are not always a result of wrongdoing. Sometimes God has a greater purpose than we can see in our suffering.

* * *

Job 15:4

But you are doing away with the fear of God and hindering meditation before God.

What does this verse say about the fear of God?

Here Eliphaz is rebuking Job again for his words. Eliphaz implies that because Job is speaking his mind and not meditating quietly, Job must not be fearing God. While Eliphaz's point may be a valid concern, he is again presumptuous of Job's heart.

* * *

Psalm 36:1

Transgression speaks to the wicked
deep in his heart; there is no fear of God
before his eyes.

What does this verse say about the fear of God?

The wicked person who has sin rooted in their heart does not fear God.

* * *

Romans 3:18

"There is no fear of God before their eyes."

What does this verse say about the fear of God?

This is a quote of Psalm 36:1 in the New Testament. In the context of this quotation, Paul is writing that both Gentiles and Jews are not righteous and do not naturally fear God.

* * *

2 Corinthians 7:1

Since we have these promises, beloved, let us cleanse ourselves from every defilement of body and spirit, bringing holiness to completion in the fear of God.

What does this verse say about the fear of God?

This verse comes right after Paul has just quoted promises from the Old Testament that summarize how God's children are to separate from evil. The promises of God and the fear of God enable us to turn away from sin and grow into mature holiness.

Appendix E: "Fears the Lord" Bible Verse Commentary

8 Verses Total:

Psalm 25:12
> Who is the man who fears the LORD?
> Him will he instruct in the way that he should choose.

What does this verse say about fearing the Lord?
> God himself instructs those who fear him.

* * *

Psalm 112:1
> Praise the LORD!
> Blessed is the man who fears the LORD,
> who greatly delights in his commandments!

What does this verse say about fearing the Lord?
> Those who fear the Lord are blessed, and they delight in what he commands.

Psalm 128:1

Blessed is everyone who fears the LORD, who walks in his ways!

What does this verse say about fearing the Lord?

Again, those who fear the Lord are blessed when they follow the paths of God.

* * *

Psalm 128:4

Behold, thus shall the man be blessed
who fears the LORD.

What does this verse say about fearing the Lord?

The verses before this communicate the principle that whoever fears the Lord will be blessed in their work and in their family.

* * *

Proverbs 14:2

Whoever walks in uprightness fears the LORD,
but he who is devious in his ways despises him.

What does this verse say about fearing the Lord?

Fearing the Lord means walking in uprightness and doing what is right. In contrast, the one who doesn't fear the Lord is devious and despises God.

APPENDIX E: "FEARS THE LORD" BIBLE VERSE COMMENTARY

* * *

Proverbs 28:14
Blessed is the one who fears the LORD always,
but whoever hardens his heart will fall into calamity.

What does this verse say about fearing the Lord?
Fearing God must be constant and ever-present, otherwise there is danger of a hardened heart toward God. Thus, neglecting to fear God will lead to calamity.

* * *

Proverbs 31:30
Charm is deceitful, and beauty is vain,
but a woman who fears the LORD is to be praised.

What does this verse say about fearing the Lord?
Fearing God is to be desired more than charm or beauty. It is a quality truly worthy of praise.

* * *

Isaiah 50:10
Who among you fears the LORD
and obeys the voice of his servant?
Let him who walks in darkness
and has no light
trust in the name of the LORD
and rely on his God.

What does this verse say about fearing the Lord?

This verse is a call for those who walk in darkness to trust in God and fear him. The surrounding verses describe the fate of those who do not fear the Lord but instead trust in their own effort.

Notes

DOES FEAR MATTER

1. Reeves, Michael. *Rejoice and Tremble: The Surprising Good News of the Fear of the Lord*. Crossway, 2021. p. 17.

2. Amirazizi, R. *America's Top Fears 2020/2021* [Data set], Chapman University, 2022, https://www.chapman.edu/wilkinson/research-centers/babbie-center/_files/Babbie%20center%20fear2021/blogpost-americas-top-fears-2020_-21-final.pdf. PDF file. Accessed 5 Apr. 2025.

3. Georges, Jayson. *The 3D Gospel: Ministry in Guilt, Shame, and Fear Cultures*. Timē Press, 2014. p. 26.

4. "Fear." *Merriam-Webster Dictionary*, Merriam-Webster, 27 Mar. 2025, www.merriam-webster.com/dictionary/fear.

5. Tozer, A. W. *The Knowledge of the Holy: The Attributes of God: Their Meaning in the Christian Life*. HarperOne, 2009. Zondervan. p. 71.

6. Lucas S. LaFreniere, Michelle G. Newman,
   Exposing Worry's Deceit: Percentage of Untrue Worries in Generalized Anxiety Disorder Treatment,
   Behavior Therapy,
   Volume 51, Issue 3,
   2020,
   Pages 413-423,
   ISSN 0005-7894,
   https://doi.org/10.1016/j.beth.2019.07.003.
   (https://www.sciencedirect.com/science/article/pii/S0005789419300826)
   Abstract: Theories of cognitive therapy have long proposed that those with generalized anxiety disorder (GAD) have inaccurate expectations. By challenging them with objective evidence, symptoms are thought to decrease. To test these premises, this study used ecological momentary assessment (EMA) during the Worry Outcome Journal (WOJ) treatment to determine the percentage of GAD worries that did not come true. We then

analyzed the association between participants' untrue worry percentages and GAD symptom change across treatment. Twenty-nine participants with GAD recorded worries when prompted for 10 days, reviewed them online nightly, and tracked their worry outcomes across 30 days. These recordings were then coded by independent raters. Analyses applied bias-correct bootstrapping path analysis on slopes extracted from longitudinal linear mixed models. Primary results revealed that 91.4% of worry predictions did not come true. Higher percentages of untrue worries significantly predicted lower GAD symptoms after treatment, as well as a greater slope of symptom reduction from pre- to post-trial. Participants' average expected likelihoods of worries coming true were much greater than actual observed likelihoods. The most common percentage of untrue worries per person was 100%. Thus, worries in those with GAD were mostly inaccurate. Greater evidence of this inaccuracy predicted greater improvement in treatment. As theorized, disconfirming false expectations may significantly contribute to treatment's effect.

Keywords: generalized anxiety disorder; worry; cognitive therapy; worry outcome monitoring; self-monitoring

7   Gibson, Padraic D. "How to Avoid Confusing the Two." *Psychology Today*, 13 June 2023, www.psychologytoday.com/us/blog/escaping-our-mental-traps/202301/whats-the-difference-between-anxiety-and-fear.

8   "Understanding Fear, Anxiety, and Phobias." *McLean Hospital*, 18 Jan. 2025, www.mcleanhospital.org/essential/fear-phobias.

9   "Five Fears." *The Spurgeon Center*, www.spurgeon.org/resource-library/sermons/five-fears. Accessed 5 Apr. 2025.

10 There are instances where Jesus tells people to not be afraid of him after they have seen his miracles or glory manifested. In these cases, Jesus is telling those around him to not have *unhealthy* fear. This type of fear is described in chapter 3. Jesus is also calming people down after experiencing the supernatural so that he can instruct them and they will be able to hear him. Jesus is in no way suggesting that we shouldn't fear God. (Matthew 14:27, 17:7, 28:10; Luke 5:10; John 6:20; Revelation 1:17-18)

A DEFINITION

11 Bridges, Jerry. *The Joy of Fearing God*. WaterBrook, 2004. p. 18.

12 McReynolds, R., and J. Bunyan. *The Fear of God in Modern English: Using the ESV as the Scripture Text*. Independently published, 2021. p. 105.

13   "7. The Fear of the Lord." *Bible.org*, www.bible.org/seriespage/7-fear-lord. Accessed 5 Apr. 2025.

FOUR FEARS

14   Allender, Dan B., and Tremper Longman. *The Cry of the Soul: How Our Emotions Reveal Our Deepest Questions about God.* 2015. pp. 83-84.

15   "Fear of God." *Jewish Encyclopedia*, www.jewishencyclopedia.com/articles/6045-fear-of-god. Accessed 5 Apr. 2025.

16   In Genesis 3:21, it is implied that the skins are animal skins, as Adam and Eve were the only humans alive at that point.

17   Bridges, Jerry. *The Joy of Fearing God.* WaterBrook, 2004. p. 103.

AWESOME GOD

18   Tozer, A. W. *The Knowledge of the Holy: The Attributes of God: Their Meaning in the Christian Life.* HarperOne, 2009. p. 104.

19   NASA. "Apollo 8: Mission Details." *NASA*, 14 Dec. 2023, www.nasa.gov/mission_pages/apollo/missions/apollo8.html.

20   NASA. "Apollo 8 Christmas Eve Broadcast." *NASA*, 25 Sept. 2007, nssdc.gsfc.nasa.gov/planetary/lunar/apollo8_xmas.html.

21   McReynolds, R., and J. Bunyan. *The Fear of God in Modern English: Using the ESV as the Scripture Text.* Independently published, 2021. p. 132.

22   *The Prince of Egypt.* Directed by Brenda Chapman, Steve Hickner, and Simon Wells, performances by Val Kilmer, Ralph Fiennes, and Michelle Pfeiffer, DreamWorks Animation, 1998.

GOD'S JUDGMENT

23   Sproul, R. C. *The Holiness of God.* Tyndale House Publishers, Inc., 1998. p. 113.

24   Chandler, Matt. *The Explicit Gospel.* Crossway, 2014. pp. 43-44.

25   Piper, John. *Desiring God: Meditations of a Christian Hedonist.* Revised ed., Multnomah, 2011, p. 58.

26   Initiative, Prison Policy. "The Research Is Clear: Solitary Confinement Causes Long-lasting Harm." *Prison Policy Initiative*, 8 Dec. 2020, www.prisonpolicy.org/blog/2020/12/08/solitary_symposium.

27   Edwards, Jonathan. *Sinners in the Hands of an Angry God.* P & R Publishing, 1992. pp. 28-29.

28 Reeves, Michael. *Rejoice and Tremble: The Surprising Good News of the Fear of the Lord*. Crossway, 2021. p. 110.

29 Sproul, R. C. *The Holiness of God*. Tyndale House Publishers, Inc., 1998. p. 175.

30 "The Wailing of Risca." *The Spurgeon Center*, www.spurgeon.org/resource-library/sermons/the-wailing-of-risca. Accessed 5 Apr. 2025.

31 Taylor, Justin. "How Much Do You Have to Hate Somebody to *Not* Proselytize?" *The Gospel Coalition*, 8 Nov. 2009, www.thegospelcoalition.org/blogs/justin-taylor/how-much-do-you-have-to-hate-somebody-to-not-proselytize.

32 Joshua, Project. "All Progress Levels." *Joshua Project*, joshuaproject.net/global/progress. Accessed 5 Apr. 2025.

THE AUTHORITY OF JESUS

33 Lewis, C. S. *The Lion, the Witch and the Wardrobe (Rack)*. HarperCollins, 2002. p. 86.

34 Tozer, A. W. *The Knowledge of the Holy: The Attributes of God: Their Meaning in the Christian Life*. HarperOne, 2009. p. 84.

36 McReynolds, R., and J. Bunyan. *The Fear of God in Modern English: Using the ESV as the Scripture Text*. Independently published, 2021. p. 17.

36 McReynolds, R., and J. Bunyan. *The Fear of God in Modern English: Using the ESV as the Scripture Text*. Independently published, 2021. p. 62.

37 Reeves, Michael. *Rejoice and Tremble: The Surprising Good News of the Fear of the Lord*. Crossway, 2021. p. 31.

38 "Five Fears." *The Spurgeon Center*, www.spurgeon.org/resource-library/sermons/five-fears. Accessed 5 Apr. 2025.

39 Bonhoeffer, Dietrich. *The Cost of Discipleship*. Touchstone, 1995. p. 89.

EMPOWERMENT OF THE SPIRIT

40 Graham, Billy. *The Holy Spirit*. Thomas Nelson, 2000. pp. 280-281.

41 Schaff, Philip. *Ante-Nicene Fathers, Volume 1: Enhanced Version* (Early Church Fathers). Christian Classics Ethereal Library, 2009, p. 139.

42 McReynolds, R., and J. Bunyan. *The Fear of God in Modern English: Using the ESV as the Scripture Text*. Independently published, 2021. p. 43.

43 Graham, Billy. *The Holy Spirit*. Thomas Nelson, 2000. pp. 129, 135, 142.

OUR FATHER'S DISCIPLINE

44 *The Lion King.* Directed by Roger Allers and Rob Minkoff, performances by Matthew Broderick, James Earl Jones, and Jeremy Irons, Walt Disney Feature Animation, 1994.

45 Spurgeon, Charles Haddon. *Classic Counsels: Soul-Stirring Topics from the Finest Messages of the Prince of Preachers.* 2003. p. 95.

46 McReynolds, R., and J. Bunyan. *The Fear of God in Modern English: Using the ESV as the Scripture Text.* Independently published, 2021. p. 50.

THE BIG PICTURE

47 *The Jesus Film.* Directed by John Krish and Peter Sykes, performances by Brian Deacon, The Jesus Film Project, 1979.

48 Bridges, Jerry. *The Joy of Fearing God.* WaterBrook, 2004. pp. 120-132.

49 The ACTS is an acronym. It is short for Adoration, Confession, Thanksgiving, Supplication. When you pray, first adore God and worship him. Then, confess your sins and your weakness. Then, thank God for things in your life and what he has done for you. Even thank him for hard things. Finally, supplicate (or ask) God for requests. These requests can be for yourself or others.

www.ingramcontent.com/pod-product-compliance
Lightning Source LLC
Chambersburg PA
CBHW070849050426
42453CB00012B/2109